The
Player's Complete Guide
to College Soccer Recruiting:

A Strategic Plan for Recruits

By

Dennis Sparks

Table of Contents

CHAPTER 1: INTRODUCTION 6

How to use this book 6

Developing and selling your soccer brand................................. 7

Give yourself the best chance to play and succeed in college soccer 8

    Be as successful as possible in the classroom............................8

    Play on the highest-level team possible where you get consistent playing time 9

    Train outside scheduled team practice................................9

    Be committed to the plan..10

    Act with dignity off the field 10

    Start taking care of your body like a professional now..............11

    Understand the nature of the college game...........................11

Email basics 12

Business analogies throughout this book 14

CHAPTER 2: OVERVIEW OF THE PROCESS 16

Major components of your footballing brand......................... 16

    Consistent performances in games 16

    How you carry yourself off the field................................16

    Email word choice and signature 17

    Player profile..17

    Highlight tape..17

    How you speak with coaches on the phone 17

    How you present yourself during visits 18

Phase 1 18

Phase 2 18

Phase 3 19

Phase 4 19

Begin the process... 20

CHAPTER 3: PHASE 1 21

Pick a major.. 21

Discover what you want in a school 22

SET A GOAL 24
    MAKE YOUR GOAL SPECIFIC.. 24
    MAKE YOUR GOAL MEASURABLE................................... 25
    MAKE YOUR GOAL ACTIONABLE 25
    MAKE YOUR GOAL RISKY.. 25
    MAKE YOUR GOAL TIMELY 26
    MAKE YOUR GOAL EXCITING...................................... 26
    MAKE YOUR GOAL RELEVANT 26
    EXAMPLE 26
IDENTIFY 100 SCHOOLS OF INTEREST THAT OFFER YOUR MAJOR 27
INITIAL EMAIL TEMPLATE... 27
SEND YOUR FIRST EMAILS TO COLLEGE COACHES 30
CHECKLIST BEFORE MOVING TO PHASE 2............................. 31

CHAPTER 4: PHASE 2 33
CRITERIA FOR PROCEEDING.. 33
REGISTER WITH THE NCAA ELIGIBILITY CENTER 33
DEVELOP YOUR PLAYER PROFILE 34
    GET A GOOD QUALITY HEADSHOT............................... 34
    INCLUDE YOUR FULL NAME 34
    INCLUDE YOUR PRIMARY AND SECONDARY POSITIONS........... 34
    INCLUDE YOUR HEIGHT AND WEIGHT 35
    PROVIDE A RELEVANT EMAIL ADDRESS 35
    PROVIDE YOUR CELL PHONE NUMBER 36
    PROVIDE YOUR NCAA ELIGIBILITY CENTER/CLEARINGHOUSE ID 36
    PROVIDE YOUR ACADEMIC BACKGROUND 36
    DETAIL YOUR CLUB SOCCER HISTORY AND ACCOMPLISHMENTS.............. 36
    DETAIL YOUR INTERNATIONAL SOCCER EXPERIENCE 37
    DETAIL YOUR HIGH SCHOOL SOCCER HISTORY AND ACCOMPLISHMENTS (IF APPLICABLE)... 38
    PROVIDE GOOD REFERENCES 39
SAMPLE PLAYER PROFILE 39
FILM YOUR MATCHES 41
EXECUTE THE PHASE 2 EMAIL STRATEGY............................. 41
PHASE 2 EMAIL #1 TEMPLATE.. 43
PHASE 2 EMAIL #2 TEMPLATE 44

Phase 2 email #3 template 45

Checklist before moving to Phase 3 46

CHAPTER 5: PHASE 3 ....**48**

Criteria for proceeding 48

Understand the importance of phase 3 49

Make a highlight tape 49

Gather footage of an entire match 52

Execute the Phase 3 email strategy 53

Talk with coaches on the phone 54

    Athletic Questions 55

    Academic Questions 56

    Campus Life Questions 57

    Financial Questions 57

Go on visits 59

Checklist before moving to Phase 4 60

CHAPTER 6: PHASE 4 ....**61**

Criteria for proceeding 61

Achieve your goal and manage your time 62

Items you need to know before you commit 62

    How much will you play? 62

    What position are you coming in to strengthen? 63

    What will be expected of you performance-wise during your time
    there? 63

    What is the Deadline of the offer? 63

    What is your total scholarship per year precisely? 64

Commit to a school 65

Take care of your body 65

    Minimize your chance of injury 65

    Eat well 66

    Train even harder 67

Set a goal for your freshman year 67

Your head coach will want to see you play again 68

Sign your letter 68

Graduate high school 69

STICK TO YOUR CONDITIONING PROGRAM 69

CHAPTER 7: OTHER ITEMS TO BE AWARE OF 70

ADAPTING THE PROCESS FOR THE WOMEN'S GAME 70

ADAPTING THE PROCESS FOR DIFFERENT CLUB AND HIGH SCHOOL SEASONS 70

DI, DII, DIII, NAIA, NJCAA, AND NCCAA SOCCER, THEIR SIMILARITIES,

AND DIFFERENCES 71

    DIVISION I.. 73

    DIVISION II... 74

    DIVISION III.. 74

    NAIA.. 75

    NJCAA 76

    NCCAA 77

TEAM CULTURE 77

INTERNATIONAL STUDENT-ATHLETES 78

CLUB TEAM RECRUITING BROCHURES.. 79

MONEY AND SCHOLARSHIPS 80

CHAPTER 8: FREQUENTLY ASKED QUESTIONS 84

WHAT PLACE DO RECRUITING QUESTIONNAIRES HAVE IN THE PROCESS? .. 84

WHAT PLACE DO COLLEGE ID CAMPS HAVE IN THE PROCESS? 84

WHAT IS MY CLUB COACH'S ROLE IN GETTING ME TO COLLEGE SOCCER? .. 85

HOW DIFFICULT IS IT TO GET A SPOT ON A COLLEGE SOCCER TEAM? 86

HOW DO I NOT COME OFF AS DESPERATE WHEN INTERACTING WITH COLLEGE

COACHES? 86

HOW DO I MANAGE HAVING MULTIPLE OFFERS WHILE STILL TALKING WITH

OTHER SCHOOLS? 88

WHAT ARE SOME COMMON MISTAKES PLAYERS MAKE WHEN

COMMUNICATING WITH COACHES? 88

SHOULD I PAY SOMEONE TO MAKE MY HIGHLIGHT TAPE?..................... 90

SHOULD A STORY OF A BAD COLLEGE SOCCER EXPERIENCE DETER ME AWAY

FROM PLAYING COLLEGE SOCCER?... 91

NOTES.. 92

MORE FROM THE AUTHOR... 93

Chapter 1:
Introduction

How to use this book

I recommend that you read the entire book before embarking on Phase 1. However, it's essential that you understand the content of the Introduction and Overview of the Process before beginning. Stephen R. Covey, author of *The 7 Habits of Highly Effective People*, states that effective people start any goal or project with its completion in mind [1]. I want you to develop a personal vision and corresponding plan for your soccer career using this book rather than blindly follow the steps outlined in this book. This is your playing career.

If you really grasp the concepts in this book then you will be able to navigate the process even when things seem uncertain or fall outside the scope of this book. You want to develop the correct way to think about recruiting and branding yourself above all else.

While reading through this book, try to visualize executing tasks with confidence, calling coaches, visiting schools, and playing under the lights in college stadiums. Additionally, reread sections of the book that are relevant to the specific phase of the recruiting process you're currently in. These phases are long enough that you will have ample opportunity to learn everything you need know to be successful in that phase.

Lastly, I want to emphasize that this book is a focused guide on how to market your footballing brand with the intent of playing to college soccer. Nothing more. Nothing less. This book is more of a plan and a strategy for approaching recruiting than an all-in-one resource for the rules of college soccer. For questions on NCAA bylaws and specific recruiting rules, you should always ask the respective compliance officers of the universities you're interested in.

Developing and selling your soccer brand

Developing and selling your brand as a soccer player is the common theme, I want you to keep in mind throughout this guide. Your brand communicates your quality, value, and style amongst many other aspects your game. Think of college coaches as your clients or partners. If you own a business, the more clients and partners you can do deals with, the greater your revenue and the greater position you have in the market. Such is the case with the prospect that is sitting on 20 offers from top division one schools. When your clients perceive your value as high and there is a market for your product (there is a large market for quality soccer players at the college level) then it's likely that your business has a great chance of being successful. Think about college recruiting this way and you will be successful in journey to college soccer.

Developing and marketing your brand is not trying to make yourself look like a much better player than you actually are. Rather, the concept of a brand seeks to clearly convey your true value as a player so coaches can easily identify you for what you actually are. College coaches should know exactly who you as a player when they interact with you in any way.

Make sure to clearly distinguish between what you want your brand to be and what it should be. What I mean in this: maybe you wish you were the center forward who is banging in goals left and right when you are, in reality, a fantastic attacking midfielder. Honestly, assess yourself as a player. At this point in your playing career, you should have a good idea of your strengths and weaknesses. If it helps, ask your coach about your best qualities. Ask him and yourself what everyone knows you for on the field.

Most players believe the myth that tons of college coaches will just find them, seek them out, and before they know it they will have tons of offers. This is true for the very best talent in the country, but not for most players. Consequently, cultivating your personal footballing brand will set you apart from the average recruit. Investing in your brand is investing in your college soccer career.

Note that coaches will define value to their program differently and emphasize the athletic, academic, social, and spiritual components of a team to different degrees. This is actually a good test to see if the program is a good fit for you. Meaning, is the coach's definition of a valuable player consistent with your definition and your brand?

The best advice I can give you for developing your brand is to be genuine and true to yourself throughout the process. Your brand should represent you. If you are sending certain signals only because that's what you think coaches want to hear, then you probably wouldn't enjoy being a part of their program anyways!

Make confidence rather than arrogance as part of your brand. Coaches love confident players but hate entitled and arrogant ones. If you communicate your brand with confidence throughout the recruiting process, coaches will be more confident that they are bringing in a valuable player to the program.

Finally, know that you will make some mistakes along the way or wish you had done something differently (this is OK and normal). Don't dwell of these moments but rather focus on the task at hand pertaining to the step you're in. Work the process!

Give yourself the best chance to play and succeed in college soccer

Be as successful as possible in the classroom

What do your grades have to do with being good enough to play college soccer? You are more attractive to a college coach if he can pay for most of your college through academics. In other words, you are a player of high value. The coach gets a lot of bang for his buck. You will be surprised how many doors this will open for you. Therefore, do as well as you possibly can in high school.

Soccer aside, your personal goal should be to graduate with as little debt as possible. Being successful in the classroom is also in your personal interest even if you never play college soccer. if you need academic support in the classroom, be proactive to get it. It may be the difference that ultimately gets you to college soccer.

Play on the highest-level team possible where you get consistent playing time

College coaches rarely come watch practices. Consequently, games are vital for being seen and ultimately getting an offer to play college soccer. Regardless how much you think you're developing as a player with your current team, you will never achieve your goal unless you are starting most games and getting significant playing time. In these prime years of player development you need to be playing and competing week in and week out.

Take a moment to think about what it communicates to college coaches if you're not playing regularly for your club team. College coaches might say to themselves something like: "If he can't get on the field for his club team how is he going to get on the field in my program?" If this is your situation currently, go to a different team.

Additionally, if you're not frequently being put under pressure in a game situation it's difficult to really mature as a player. There are so many players that are great in practice but go missing when they get their chance on the field. You want to be known for showing up when it really matters.

Train outside scheduled team practice

The bottom line is that your team should be training at least three times a week. If this is not the case, something is wrong with the philosophy of your club or coach, and you need to find a new team. Nevertheless, even three times a week is not enough. You should look to touch the ball six days a week most weeks of the year. It is always a good idea to take one day off per week to allow your body to rest.

All the best players in the world have risen to top in part because of the amount of quality time they have spent with the ball over a period of years. This is a huge part of your development and delivering consistent performances on the pitch. Also, look for another person of higher skill level to train with in order to accelerate your improvement and keep you accountable.

Be committed to the plan

Just as with anything worthwhile in life, results come when you put in the work. Don't get discouraged if several emails or interactions with coaches don't go as you expect (this will inevitably happen at some point). Keep going with the process. The difference between you achieving your goal and not achieving your goal could be as simple as your perseverance.

Hard work is like compound interest. That is, sometimes you don't see great results in the beginning but later down the road you will shock yourself for what you will be able to accomplish. Your frequent investments of hard work will result in greater results than your competition, even if they started ahead of you.

If you have a clear vision for your soccer career, staying committed will not be difficult. Let this direction be the central force that orients your actions and commitment throughout the recruiting process and your entire career.

Act with dignity off the field

I cannot tell you number of players that I knew personally that would have played for big Division I programs if it hadn't been for their struggles with alcohol, drugs, and other distractions. I'm sure you may know several players that fit this narrative.

Stories like these actually break my heart because so many talented players fail to reach their potential and they can't get time back. The only reason I bring this up is to emphasize that what you do off the pitch is just as important (if not more) as what you do on the pitch.

Furthermore, your behavior and character off the field is often the first thing a college coach will ask your club coach about you because trouble kids are bad investments for coaches. Think about it. Coaches spend lots of time and money to bring them in and it's more likely that they will not last four years when compared to a player who knows how to make good decisions in his personal life. Additionally, it reflects poorly on coaches when they bring trouble into their program and the university.

The great part about your actions off the field is that you have 100% control of them. This should be a given for every player aspiring to play college soccer.

Start taking care of your body like a professional now

Unfortunately, this is something that prospective student-athletes and college players alike do very poorly. If you start taking care of your body early on, you will be less likely to get injured. If you're less likely to be injured, you're also less likely to miss big showcases and events where college coaches recruit. Forgetting college soccer for a moment, I believe every player wants to stay as injury free as possible so that they can play, train, and develop as much as possible.

Moreover, one of the best attributes a player can have is consistent availability. We have all known extremely talented players who have struggled with many injuries over the years and have missed a lot of minutes in games. You don't want to be this to be a part of your soccer brand!

Understand the nature of the college game

There are a handful of characteristics of the college game you need to understand. Understanding these items will ultimately help you build your brand. These are:

High pace of play

The pace of play in college soccer is significantly quicker than that of high-level club matches. The ball is always moving faster whether it's in the air or on the pitch. Passes are drilled into players' feet, diagonal balls are almost always driven, players are punished for dwelling on the ball too long, and decisions have to be made very quickly. This forces new college players to think very rapidly and most importantly, know what they want to do with the ball long before they get it.

Physicality

As I alluded to above, college soccer is extremely physical. By this I generally am referring to two things; namely speed/quickness and strength/aggressiveness. Forwards and center backs are generally very fast. Meaning, if you're the type of player who solely relies on beating players with speed, you might struggle once you get to college soccer. Additionally, players are stronger and more aggressive on both sides of the ball. Center forwards have the ability to hold up the ball and use their bodies to create space for chances on goal. Midfielders and defenders will hit you just about every opportunity you give them and are experienced in committing professional fouls when needed. This encourages new college players to get stronger and adapt their game to become more aggressive sooner rather than later.

Direct style

College soccer teams on average play very direct rather than building up play patiently. Even the teams that keep the ball on the ground tend to play more direct. For example, a team might get the ball into the forward's feet as often as possible and try to get other players forward by playing off of him. Other teams unapologetically bypass the midfield consistently via long flighted balls. The latter types of teams tend to be particularly physical. This aspect of college soccer will only really affect you if your college coach asks you to do something you might not typically have done with your club side.

Keeping these three guarantees of college soccer in mind, you can start to prepare yourself for the college game before you even get there. Reflect on your style of play and determine how you can improve when it comes to pace of play and physicality. Half of your improvement these two areas just simply comes down to changing your mentality when you step on the field. Make a conscious decision everyday to know what you're going to do with the ball before you get and play with aggression and intensity.

Email basics

Most of your correspondence with college coaches, especially in the beginning, will take place via email. Consequently, becoming professional at communicating through email is absolutely vital to your success in the college recruiting process. I want to briefly go over some of the basic concepts you need to understand about emailing college coaches so you can avoid some common mistakes and start to form a good framework for structuring emails.

First and foremost, make sure your email address is appropriate and professional. I think the best way to explain this concept is through some examples. Examples of inappropriate email addresses include:

- jackisabeast@example.com
- pimptom@example.net
- gunner4life@example.org
- dantheman@exmaple.com

Examples of appropriate emails include:

- jackbrown22@example.com
- davidhjohnson@example.com
- richardjames2019@example.net
- thortonjames@example.com

Your email address should contain your first and last name (spelled correctly) with optional numbers, periods, and underscores. A college coach should be able to easily identify who you are just by looking at your email address. If he can't, then your email address fails to identify you.

If you have been using an inappropriate email address up until now, you need to make a new account with an appropriate address before moving forward with the process.

The next thing I recommend when it comes to composing emails is to get some sort of browser plugin that acts as a spellchecker. Otherwise, you are bound to make a grammatical error at some point. A great example of such a tool is Grammerly, which I generally have had really experiences with. You should also know that some college coaches will disregard your email altogether if blatant errors exist, especially if it is the first email you send them. An email full of errors communicates that you did not care enough to take a few more minutes to proof read your email.

Additionally, you should have a professional headshot for your account's profile image so that coaches can associate a face with your name. After sending several emails, this association should become automatic for them. If you do not have a good headshot, I would recommend asking around your various circles to see if someone would be willing to do it for you. You could also suggest to your team manager that all players get professional headshot as a team.

Lastly, you should create a professional looking email signature for you account. Make sure your signature is consistent with your footballing brand. Your signature should include your full name, email address, cell phone number, and some sort of title that identifies you as a player. Such a title could be something like "Center Forward, Atlanta United Academy U16". See below for a full example. Regardless of how you choose to structure your signature, make sure it's not distracting, elaborate, or flashy. You don't want it to take away from the actual content of your email.

Joe Brown

Center Forward, Atlanta United Academy U16

JBrown@example.com

(XXX) XXX-XXX

Atlanta, GA

Email continues to prove itself as an essential skill that all prospects must master for effective communication. The more you develop your ability to write good emails the easier the recruiting process will be for you.

Business analogies throughout this book

Business is a very popular major for college students, especially student athletes. Many of you may already know something about or have an interest in business so my goal here is to teach you a little about business along the way to aid in many of the branding concepts that are taught in this book.

College soccer is the industry you operate in and you specialize in what you do best as a soccer player. College programs don't have unlimited budgets so those players that market their brand the best will have an advantage in the market. **Figure 1** below shows the Circular Flow Diagram of College Soccer. One could depict this for any industry but this is a good overview of how money and resources travel in college soccer.

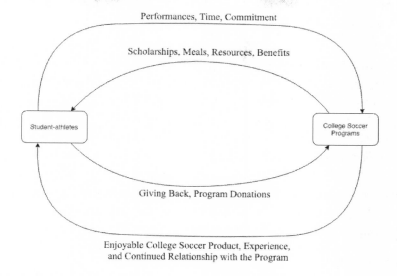

Figure 1: Circular Flow Diagram of College Soccer

Notice that the inside arrows involve money while the outer arrows involve services and other desirables. College soccer program give money to student-athletes mainly in the form of scholarships while student-athletes give the school their tuition and the program their donations after graduating. Similarly, players give their time and performances in exchange for an enjoyable experience.

What does your brand have to do with **Figure 1**? Coaches want to know if you can give them good performances and commitment if they are going to provide you a good experience and scholarship money. Develop your brand such that you first show what you can give to a program with rather than focusing on what you can receive first. As you can see above, college soccer hinges on this dynamic.

Whether you actually own a business or work in a corporate setting at some point down the road (this will be almost all of you), learning how to be professional in the recruiting process will undoubtedly benefit you in your future endeavors. Don't worry about not understanding the concepts in this book if you don't have any interest in business since everything is also spelled out plainly for your convenience.

Chapter 2:
Overview of the Process

Before looking at the different steps of the recruiting process, I want to take some time to go over the larger items that make up your soccer brand. Note that these different components are spread out over the four phases of plan.

Major components of your footballing brand

Consistent performances in games

Players should strive to make consistency an integral part of their brand. You want your club coach telling college coaches that you're always on time, always display your talents during games, and that the team can always look to you for reliability.

Furthermore, college coaches will drop you in an instant if you're not consistent. Club coaches tend not to do this nearly as much. The reason behind this is that college coaches must win to keep their jobs while this is generally not the case for youth coaches.

More than the fact that consistency is an attractive characteristic to college coaches, you should desire it as a mechanism to better yourself in all walks of life. I would argue that learning to be disciplined in achieving consistency is one of the most important life skills that soccer can teach you because it molds your character to perform even when things are difficult.

How you carry yourself off the field

I have already touched on this in Chapter 1 so I won't spend much time here, but this spans everything from your personal decisions to your confidence and posture in public places. Your repeated choices in this department accumulate into how your brand is perceived.

Email word choice and signature

Email word choice is a big deal because it gives coaches a glimpse of your personality and thought processes. You have a great opportunity to convey professionalism just by choosing your words wisely.

On the other hand, your email signature is not a huge part of your brand but is a nice touch that college coaches will consistently see. It helps remind them more frequently about who you are and your value as a player.

Player profile

This is an important part of your brand because it details where you have been, and what you have accomplished to date. Consequently, college coaches will use such information to help determine where you are going in your career and if their program will be a part of it.

By taking the time to put together a player profile, you are telling coaches that you respect their time enough to give them a quick reference for your entire career. You will explore this aspect of your brand more in Phase 2.

Highlight tape

While highlight videos are not emphasized as much in soccer as it is in football and other sports, I believe your brand can benefit tremendously from a solid highlight reel. Many players will not have tape put together so this will be something that allows you to stand out.

This aspect of your brand requires lots of effort on the front end in order to just capture the footage; however, the potential reward for having good highlight tape is significant.

How you speak with coaches on the phone

In a similar fashion to your word choice in email, you have an opportunity to present yourself as a professional except in a more personal light. That is, coaches will remember your phone conversations more than they remember an exchange of emails.

Conceptually, this component can be thought of as a part of how you carry yourself off the field, but since it has the potential to be so impactful, I thought it was worth mentioning specifically.

How you present yourself during visits

Again, this is similar to the last component but is even more personal because it involves you and coaches face-to-face. Projecting confidence when speaking to coaches, faculty, current players in the program, how you dress, your degree of eye contact, and the energy you convey to others all greatly contribute to a successful visit and presentation of your soccer brand.

Phase 1

In Phase 1, you will discover your interests and learn what you want from a school academically, athletically, geographically, socially and spiritually. You will learn to set an ultimate goal for the recruiting process and how to begin your strategy for emailing coaches. Finally, you will learn useful tips on how to manage and catalog the status of your dialogue with schools of interest.

Phase 1 sets a firm foundation that allows you be successful for the remainder of the plan. It is normal to feel like the work you do in Phase 1 isn't amounting to much. Remember, you are just starting to develop your brand at this point. Throughout Phase 1 you will mature just as much in the recruiting process as you do on the pitch.

Phase 2

In this second step, you will start to flesh out your brand more while beginning some more meaningful communication with the coaches from schools on your list. Furthermore, you will start to set some of the groundwork for Phase 3 and mature your email strategy. In this stage, you should start to see some of the fruits of your labor. However, don't be tempted to stop your hard work at this point. Phase 3 is a crucial step in achieving your goal.

Phase 2 is when the prospect starts sensing that contacts and conversations with coaching staffs are becoming more serious. It should become progressively clearer to the prospective student-athlete that things will come to a head eventually. Many players are also in the process of finishing their physical maturation during this time, so it's natural for this period to feel like a significant transition overall.

Phase 3

This is the most important step in the entire recruiting process, especially for boys. The bulk of college recruiting is done during the prospect's junior year. In this phase, you will take a huge step in communicating your brand by putting together a highlight tape and footage of an entire game. After reading about Phase 3, you'll be able to continue executing your email strategy, know how to talk to college coaches on the phone, and how to approach school visits. Furthermore, you will learn how to land offers with your visits and prepare to make a good decision for your commitment.

Phase 3 can easily extend into the beginning of your senior year depending on the prior work you've put in and your particular situation. It's not unheard of for most of your visits to take place during the beginning of your senior year. However, keep in mind that, generally, the earlier you start going on visits, the more options you will have.

Phase 4

In this step, you will learn how achieve the goal you set in phase 1 and how to manage the time between your initial commitment and when you arrive on campus. Moreover, you will learn to identify important milestones during this time period and how to navigate them wisely.

There are many instances of prospects that have done well enough to secure a commitment to a school but ultimately throw it away with their behavior prior to arriving on campus. Your decisions in Phase 4 are just as impactful as your prior work in the process. Phase 4 is all about equipping you to sprint through the finish line.

Begin the process

Having grasped the vision for your recruiting process and learned some basic concepts, you're now ready to begin your journey as a prospective student-athlete. Remember that your voyage and ultimate arrival at your destination hinges on your effort and attitude throughout the process. A good beginning starts you farther ahead than those who you are competing with for a place in college soccer.

I want to encourage you to remind yourself continually about the vision you have for yourself in soccer. Every journey worth beginning will have at least some major setbacks. However, keeping your vision and goals in mind will sustain you through the ups and downs that are guaranteed to come with the recruiting process. You can do it!

Chapter 3:
Phase 1

Remember that the groundwork is done in Phase 1 so that the focus can be progressively more on meaningful communication with coaches. This meaningful communication comes later on in the process but it won't come unless you have the plan to succeed and actually act on that plan. You need not get frustrated when instant results don't come your way. If you stick with the process, results will come.

A major part of Phase 1 is discovering your interests, which will ultimately inform what you want to do personally and professionally over the next ten years of your life. Thinking through aspects of the college recruiting process early on gives you some time to change your direction if you're interests change during your time in high school. It's absolutely normal for your interests change during this period. Many times kids try something that they think they would enjoy but end up hating it. For example, I was playing for a semi-professional team one summer during undergrad and had a sales job that had flexible hours around my training schedule. I only did this job for about three months but it didn't take me long to realize that I didn't enjoy cold calling and asking for the sale as much I enjoyed other subjects. This experience informed me that I wasn't too interested in consumer sales.

Pick a major

Going off the above discussion regarding interests, you first must understand that picking a major doesn't make sense without some sort of career in mind. That is, a college education is a means to an end rather than the end itself. This doesn't relate much to college soccer but it will be hugely impactful on the rest of your life.

If you don't know where to start researching different careers and industries, I would recommend checking out the Bureau of Labor Statistics Occupational Outlook Handbook (OOH). The OOH categorizes careers by their industry and presents statistics as well as descriptions for these categories and the jobs they're comprised of. Statistics you'll find on the OOH include projected percent increase and average salary to name a few.

Going in as undecided for your major is futile, especially if you are paying a significant portion of your expenses out of pocket. Yes, college is an investment, but an investment gives you a return, and being undecided for the first two years of college won't give you the greatest return. It's better to have a plan and then change that plan if new information comes up. Undecided communicates the lack of a plan.

Discover what you want in a school

When determining what you want in a school that could be your athletic and academic home for four years, there are several important exercises to go through. First, ask yourself the following:

What types of schools am I interested in attending?

This first question is quite broad and deals with many different groups of criteria for schools. These groups are: **school funding**, **degree-type** (2/4 year), **gender**, **religious affiliation**, **geography**, and **size**. There may be some other groupings that come to mind during your reflection; however, these cover the most important characteristics for any school.

Below is an example of selecting desired criteria for each group. Keep in mind that this is only an example. Note that the checks have been placed arbitrarily.

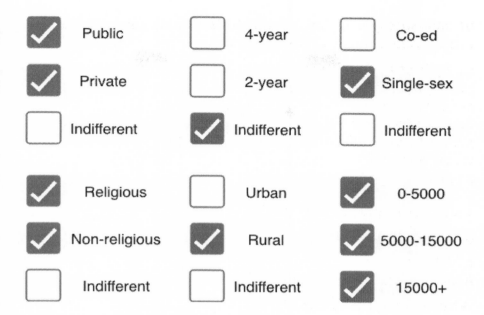

Figure 2: Criteria to Judge Schools By

Also, note that being indifferent is not the same as checking every other box for that group. Indifferent indicates that you don't have a preference while checking all other boxes indicates that you would be interested in attending those types of schools.

The next question is a more focused extension of the previous exercise; however, it deserves some thought due to the plethora of choices in and the size of the United States.

What states would I enjoy living in?

While asking yourself this question think about climate, culture, economic opportunity, distance from home, distance from other relatives, and other geographical criteria in order to inform your decision.

Initially, choose ten states that you would enjoy living in during your time in college. Keep in mind that different states have different kinds and different numbers of programs so don't think that you can't consider programs that aren't located in these ten states. This is simply an exercise to discover your preferences.

Next:

Order the following components by their relative importance

Degree Value (Academic/Financial)

Athletic

Location

Social

Spiritual

Order these components of your college decision with rankings 1-5. That is, 1 is your most important aspect for a school while 5 is your least important aspect. I have put the Academic and Financial components together because they together determine the value of your degree. That is, you can think about your degree's value using the following formula:

$$Degree\ Value = \frac{Quality\ of\ Education}{Cost\ of\ Education}$$

I don't necessarily recommend calculating an actual number for each school you're interested. Rather, this is just a way to think about the value and return on investment your degree will provide.

Set a goal

After you have completed the above exercises and are somewhat confident with the understanding of your interests, you need to set a goal for the recruiting process. Goal setting is something people generally struggle with; however, by just setting a goal you will gain a huge leg up on your competition. However, the most important thing about setting a goal is to make sure it's SMARTER [2].

Make your goal specific

Your goal must be specific. Vague goals are relative and don't inspire you to take action. For example, "I want to become a better soccer player" is not a goal but rather a desire. When it comes to the recruiting process, your goal could include things like the style the program plays, maybe the conference you want to play in, etc.

Additionally, focus your goal on criteria that deals with soccer. Don't add too many dimensions to your goal statement so that it turns into a paragraph. You want your goal to be concise enough to look at and immediately invoke the image of where you will be in the future.

Make your goal measurable

Your goal must be measurable. If you goal is not measurable, how can you determine if you have achieved your goal? You want to be able to look back and say confidently that you achieved my goal because you sold 350 memberships this year, for example.

For the recruiting process, there are two ways you can think about this. First, at the deadline of your goal you can ask yourself "Did I make it to the collegiate level?", "Did I hit my financial number for the cost of school?", etc. However, you should also measure your progress along the way on a daily or weekly basis. For example, say you devote a minimum of 2 hours a week working on the recruiting process. You can obviously measure the time but your tasks should also be measurable. Sending three emails of distinct content at three specific times during your season is a great example of a measurable task that will help you achieve your ultimate goal.

Make your goal actionable

Your goal must be actionable. I hinted at this above when discussing measurable goals, but it is essential that goals can be acted upon. In fact, that's probably the reason you are reading this book. Reading this book is a great first step but if players don't actually execute the plan then they don't really have a goal. Michael Hyatt in his book *Your Best Year Ever* puts it simply when says, "Goals are fundamentally about what you're going to do." [2].

Make your goal risky

Your goal must be risky. I understand that this may seem odd; however, goals that are too realistic are not worth striving for. That is, the more difficult the goal the more meaningful it becomes [2]. The fact that you are setting out to play college soccer is by nature risky because of some the things you will have to sacrifice along the way.

Also keep in mind that risky can mean different things to difficult people. One player might strive to play Division I at all costs while another might strive to play college soccer while studying pre-med.

Make your goal timely

Your goal must be timely. That is, put a time limit on your goal. Deadlines are motivation and prevent you from indefinite procrastination.

When it comes to recruiting, I recommend that you pursue a verbal commitment time of either late in their junior year or during the first semester of their senior year. However, you need to pick a specific date during this window that is specific for your situation.

Make your goal exciting

Your goal must be exciting! If your goal doesn't excite you when you dream about achieving it then you need a new goal. Again exciting will mean different things to different players. One player might get excited about playing soccer at a big school in a big city in front of a big crowd while another might get excited about playing for the college in his hometown.

Make your goal relevant

Your goal must be relevant. How important is playing college soccer to you? If it only merits moderate importance then setting a goal to play Division I soccer in the ACC probably doesn't make too much sense. As I've mentioned before you need to adapt the process to your specific situation. In other words, make it relevant for you.

Example

Here is an example of a SMARTER goal:

To verbally commit and contribute to an ACC program that looks to play high pressure, penetrating soccer by May 15th of my junior year of high school.

Most importantly, you must write this goal down [2]. Write it down multiple times. Even write it down once a day. Secondly, put your written goal in a place where you will see it every single day, possibly even multiple times a day. You need to visualize the end to your means. Reading that goal and visualizing living that goal every single day should invoke the excitement of getting to the next level. Once your goal is written down, practice speaking it out loud every single day to affirm your vision for your playing career.

Lastly, make sure your goal has a why behind it. What is your motivation for forming this goal? Is it to play professional soccer? Is it to be the first person in your family to attend college? Is it because you love the game? Could such an opportunity change your life and lives of your family members? You should spend some time reflecting on this question before jumping into the next section.

Identify 100 schools of interest that offer your major

At this point you should have a good understanding of what you want in a school and your ultimate destination for the recruiting process. You need to identify 100 schools of interest based on the criteria you have outlined. You can easily type this list up in either Excel or Word.

Note that all 100 schools don't have to satisfy 100% of the criteria you outlined at the beginning of this phase (this is pretty much impossible); however, every school should posses most of these characteristics. This is not to say that you cannot consider schools that meet less than half of your criteria. You just need to have clear in your mind those items that you won't compromise on. In fact, this will most likely come about when a school that's not on your list initiates contact with you.

Generally, you want to keep your options open within reason. Obviously you cannot keep all options open indefinitely (offers have deadlines for example). Don't think of this as a hard and fast list but rather a starting point to kick-start your communication with college coaches.

Initial email template

Now that you have identified 100 potential schools of interest, it's time to take some action and send initial emails out. However, you need to have a plan for what to say when you make your first impression to coaches. Below is the template you will use to reach out to coaches. You should understand the following about the template before using it:

Notice that the template is highly specific to you as a player, and therefore, requires you to fill in the parts in parentheses. You will certainly be able to fill in the majority of these blanks off the top of your head, but some of them will require you to look some information up.

Also note that there is nothing special about this template. In fact, it's pretty standard and basic in terms of its format. However, it hits all basic introductory items and is professional in its formulation. Additionally, you don't want to send coaches everything about your career in the first email. The emphasis should be on wanting to know more about the program and establishing a relationship.

Go ahead and study the template below. Make sure to look over it at least a couple of times before jumping to the next section where the email strategy is detailed.

Coach (Insert Coach's Last Name),

      Hope all is well. My name is *(Insert Your Full Name)*, and I'm wrapping up my freshman year at *(Insert High School)* in *(Insert High School Location)*. I am interested in *(Insert Name of School)*'s soccer program. I realize college is a few years away, but still wanted to learn more about your program. Let me give you a brief bio of my playing career:

- (Insert Your Previous Team with Year and Level)
- (Insert Your Previous Team Stats and Accomplishments)
- (Insert Your Current Team with Year and Level)
- (Insert Your Current Team Stats and Accomplishments)
- (Insert Any Other Relevant Career Information)

In this upcoming fall season, I will be playing for the (Insert Team Name, Club, and Level). I am a (Insert Descriptive Adjective Consistent with Your Brand) player, but my main position is (Insert Position). I am known for my (List a Few Things That You Do Very

Well on the Field). Academics are also very important to me. I finished my freshman year with a GPA of (Insert GPA). (State Your Class Rank if Available/Applicable).

Feel free to contact any of the following coaches regarding myself: (Insert Name and Title of First Coach) at (Insert First Coach's Number), (Insert Name and Title of Second Coach) at (Insert Second Coach's Number), (Insert Name and Title of Third Coach) at (Insert Third Coach's Number). Thank you.

Sincerely,

(Insert Your Name)

Now that you have somewhat of a framework to think about sending your first emails, you should understand a few do's and don'ts when it comes to every email you'll send:

Do

- Address the coach
- Have a standard greeting (i.e. something to the effect of "Hope all is well.")
- Make sure your email signature looks good and is working

Don't

- Be overly informal or unprofessional
- Rush sending emails (typing errors reflect really poorly on you)

Remember to look over your email at least two or three times before sending it. When you send an email with several spelling errors, it communicates to that coach that you didn't care enough to spend an extra minute reviewing your email (i.e. this email really wasn't that important to you).

This may sound a bit extreme, but the small details can matter in these types of things, especially when it comes to first impressions. Take the extra minute; it's worth it!

Send your first emails to college coaches

You will now send your first emails to college coaches using the initial email template. Take the time to fill in the blanks carefully, put the head coach as the recipient and carbon copy any assistants. Most importantly, remember that this serves as a first impression to college coaches. Take as much time as you need to make sure no spelling errors or unfilled blanks remain. Few things turn college coaches off more than multiple obvious typing mistakes in your first email.

The timing of this first email is also important. Some would say that freshman year is too early to start emailing coaches; however, emailing them later in your semester of your freshman year lets coaches know you're interested and thinking ahead without seeming desperate and over ambitious.

Specifically, you should send modified versions of the initial template email to all 100 schools on your list between the months of March and April (100 total emails). If you are not used to sending many emails this may seem daunting. However, remember that it's still early in the recruiting process. There's no need to rush.

Sending these emails out early on is effective because when someone shows interest in someone else, it is more likely to result in that person reciprocating interest as well.

Again, you should address the head coach in your letter but copy all assistant coaches. Now, where would one find the head and assistant coaches' emails? Sometimes their contact info will be with their bio in the coaches section of the website; however, most of the time you will have to look under Staff Directory. Staff Directory can usually be found by looking under the "Inside Athletics" tab on the site's main navigation bar. Some universities make you hunt coaches' contact info down.

Another reason that timing is important for this first email is because college coaches have more time to attend to emails in the spring because they are not in season (coaches' hours with the team are limited by the NCAA during the out of season period). Moreover, they will be planning to travel to watch players over the spring, summer, and following fall so their mind will already be geared in this direction.

Throughout the recruiting process, it's a good idea to document where you're at for your own benefit. One way to do this from the beginning is by adding a second column to your list of 100 that indicates if the coach responded to you. Go ahead and put tick marks there as responses come in. This is easy to do in Microsoft Excel or another program.

In response, college coaches will typically thank you for your interest in the program and ask you to stay in touch because you've started so early. This is perfectly fine. Make sure to give coaches until the end of May to respond to your initial email so you can mark them as responding on your list. By June your mind should already be thinking about moving to Phase 2 and coaches are unlikely to respond past May if they haven't already.

Also, they may ask you to send them your club soccer schedule for the upcoming season once it's released. Be prepared to send it them as soon as you have it but also follow up with them right before the season begins (this is discussed in the next chapter). With all that said, you should never get caught up in a coach's initial response. The purpose of this first email is only to establish a connection that could pave the way for future communication.

Checklist before moving to Phase 2

At this point you've learned everything you need to know about Phase 1 and are ready to take on Phase 2. Make sure you've completed the following steps in Phase 1 before moving on to anything in Phase 2. Go back and review certain sections as needed. If a particular step in Phase 1 isn't going well, I encourage you to go back and read that section again. In particular, look for the part of the step where things start to fall apart. All the small details count in the recruiting process.

Phase 1 Checklist

- ✓ Pick a major
- ✓ Outline your interests
- ✓ Set a SMARTER goal

- ✓ Send your first 100 emails to schools on your initial list
- ✓ Narrow down your list to 50 schools

Note that I have added a task to this list. In between Phase 1 and Phase 2, you should narrow down your initial list of schools in order to prepare for Phase 2. Specifically, narrow down your list to 50 schools based on your interests, responses from coaches, continued research, personal reflection, priorities, and intuition.

Note that just because a coach didn't respond doesn't mean you can't keep their program on your narrowed list. Coaches get so many emails and they very well may respond to your next email. The key is to be persistent and committed to opportunities to communicate without being annoying or seeming desperate, of course.

At this point in the recruiting process, there is no reason to be desperate. Work the process. You should be developing your own game so well that coaches should be desperate to have you in their program. Change your thinking in order to change your results.

Chapter 4:
Phase 2

Phase 2 is an essential phase for developing your brand as an emerging soccer player. Consequently, many players start to see some results in terms of interest from schools in Phase 2. However, don't let this slow down the momentum you have been building so far in the recruiting process.

Think of the recruiting process like a great story with a clear climax. The climax of the recruiting process happens during Phase 4 of the recruiting process and everything is building up until the moment you commit in early Phase 4. That is, if you don't continue with the same drive, you'll never reach the climax.

Criteria for proceeding

Again, make sure you have picked a major, outlined your interests, formulated a goal, sent your emails, and narrowed down your list to 50 schools before proceeding past this point.

Take a quick peek at the end of the previous chapter in case you need a more detailed reminder of any of these items. The order of the different tasks presented throughout this book is very important.

Register with the NCAA Eligibility Center

The NCAA Eligibility Center (formerly called the NCAA Clearinghouse) is the medium by which the NCAA tracks student athletes and makes sure they are eligible. This is accomplished by submitting various academic documents and providing data on your previous playing experience.

Registering with the NCAA Eligibility Center is required before any student-athlete arrives on campus as a freshman. Consequently, since this isn't the most glamorous part of the recruiting process, it's good to get it over with now. Moreover, coaches often will ask you if you've registered for the Eligibility Center. You want to make your life easy so you can answer yes to this question every time.

33

Getting these sort of tasks out of the way allows you to focus more of your time later on genuine communication with coaches. Time is always more valuable a little bit later in the process because it's closer to when you will commit.

Develop your player profile

Developing a player profile is one of the major components of your footballing brand and a necessary piece for a successful Phase 2. Coaches will initially gauge you based on a fairly small subset of information so it's important for you to take control of how your brand is seen amongst college coaches.

Essentially, your player profile gives coaches a summary of you, where you've been, where you want to go, what your strengths are, and what's important to you in soccer. If you can create a positive initial impression for a coach it can really go a long way. In short, the player profile for the prospects is the balance sheet for a business. It takes a cumulative view rather than taking a picture during a moment in time.

Below I detail all the items that makeup a good and complete player profile. Refer back to this section often when you're actually constructing the document you plan to send to coaches.

Get a good quality headshot

A professional headshot makes your face familiar for coaches in emails, and serves to complement your brand on the field. There is simply just something about a high quality photo where the person is well put together.

Include your full name

Provide your full name in big, bold print on your player profile so that it is easy to see.

Include your primary and secondary positions

Stating your primary and secondary position communicates to the coach that you know where you would be of most value to his/her program. Furthermore, coaches always have more urgent positions of need for each recruiting class. By providing your primary and secondary position in a clear format, coaches can quickly determine if you meet an immediate need of the program.

You should be as specific as possible when listing your positions. For example, you shouldn't put forward as your primary position and midfielder as your secondary position. These are too vague as they span several actual positions. A better example would be listing your primary and secondary positions as a wide right-sided forward and attacking midfielder (#10), respectively.

Lastly, you need to decide how your position fits into your overall brand. That is, you should know who you are as a player and what your best position is. If you're not specific and intentional about this, college coaches will likely make assumptions about where you play and therefore how you play. It may even lead them to think of you as a utility player. This is not to say that being a utility player is a bad thing; it's certainly not. However, if you're already known as a utility player but would rather not be one, it's really difficult to change the perceptions of coaches and players alike. By being intentional about how you communicate your positioning during the recruiting process, you put yourself in a position to influence perceptions at the beginning of your relationship with a coach.

Include your height and weight

As mentioned previously, college soccer tends to be a more physical brand of soccer. Whether it's right or wrong, some coaches will make some basic judgments of you just based on your height and weight. This may work in your favor or against you depending on several factors. Either way, it's good to present this information up front so you can see how important it is for different coaches.

Provide a relevant email address

At this point you've already sent your initial email to coaches you plan on staying in contact with. Make sure to use that same email address as the address you provide on your player profile. You never want to make coaches guess which email address they should reach you at. Furthermore, it makes communication really easy to manage on your end as everything is in one place.

Provide your cell phone number

Provide your cell number clearly for coaches to reference. This number together with your email address will be the primary mediums through which you will communicate with coaches. If you do not have a cell number, there are a number of other ways you can make calls through via the Internet, but just make sure to communicate this to coaches if this is your situation.

Provide your NCAA Eligibility Center/Clearinghouse ID

Providing your NCAA Eligibility Center ID shows coaches that you're already on top of registering with Eligibility Center and provides it for their convenience. If talks become advanced between you and a particular program, coaches may go ahead and send that ID to their compliance officer.

Provide your academic background

It's important to tell coaches the essential components of your academic profile. These include your cumulative GPA, standardized test scores (if you've taken them), the number of college credits earned, and other significant academic accomplishments. You may have not completed any college-level coursework at this point, and that's OK.

You should refrain from including more academic information in excess of the above items. It would appear a bit strange to coaches if your player profile contained more academic information than athletic information. Additionally, coaches usually know enough to give you a quick estimate of the amount of academic aid you would be given just based on your cumulative GPA and test scores, making them a no brainer to include in your player profile.

Detail your club soccer history and accomplishments

This undoubtedly should be the most important and largest section of your player profile. Again, coaches really value what you do at the high levels of club soccer rather than your accomplishments with your high school. This section of your player profile should contain the following:

- Every team (with level) you played for since you freshman year with years
- Trophies won with years
- Any statistics you may have from your teams (GP, GS, G, A, etc.)
- Finishes in top national tournaments with years

Make it point to let coaches know if you've played at a particularly higher level such as the United States Soccer Development Academy (USSDA) or the Olympic Development Program (ODP). Just to clarify, examples of top tournaments include but are not limited to Disney Showcase, Dallas Cup, and Surf Cup.

Be very detailed and specific in this section so that there's no confusion when it comes to your most important athletic accomplishments. Work on this section over in several sitting to make sure you've not accidentally omitted anything essential. If you don't have access to statistics from past seasons, you may want to see if a volunteer could keep some basic stats for your team. However, in many higher levels, stats are kept through the league and are published online for all to see.

Detail your international soccer experience

International soccer experience for most youth players in the United States comes in two forms; namely, trials with foreign clubs and trips overseas with a club or ODP team. Since it's fairly expensive to pursue these opportunities, many prospects will not be able to have this section in their player profile.

However, if you're fortunate enough to have gone overseas to play the game, then your player profile will stand out. However, while international soccer experience is beneficial, know that it will not suddenly make college coaches aggressively recruit you.

You will find that your experiences playing soccer overseas will be a great conversation starter once you do speak to coaches over the phone. Many programs take team trips abroad periodically so many coaches will genuinely be interested in your experience in a given part of the world.

Detail your high school soccer history and accomplishments (If applicable)

This section will apply to some of you and not to others, as some of the more elite club leagues prevent their players from participating in high school soccer. For many players, high school soccer is a big deal and something they care deeply about. While college coaches usually don't share this view, outstanding statistics from your high school seasons certainly won't hurt your brand when it comes to getting recruited. Nevertheless, this section of your player profile should contain any of the following:

- Seasons with years, statistics, and position played
- Any awards or accolades
- Description of playoff run for each year

If you've transferred high schools, make it explicitly clear which school is associated with which season and year. It's not uncommon for prospective student-athletes to transfer high schools just to play on a higher quality team or have a chance to win a state championship. Additionally, you may have noticed the inclusion of your position above. The reason is because players often play a different (usually more advanced) position with their high school teams. Now, this may seem contradictory to my comments on the position section of your player profile; however, coaches always want to bring in a player who can contribute with goals, regardless of position.

For example, say you undoubtedly see yourself a center back, but score at least 20 goals every high school season playing forward. Rather than confusing college coaches, this will likely tell them you have some potential in the opposition's box. Consequently, they may view you as the type of center-back who could score one or two goals a season off of set pieces.

Awards and accolades in high school soccer include recognition such, All-county, all-district, all-region, all-state, etc. While these ultimately don't mean too much to college coaches, it's still worth including on your player profile.

Lastly, when detailing playoff runs something as simple as state quarterfinalist or state runner-up would suffice. However, you can give a little bit more detailed description if the season or accomplishment needs to be explained further.

Provide good references

You need to provide trusted references in your player profile just as many people do on their resume. Three relevant references should be your goal. Furthermore, of the three there will certainly be one that comes to mind first. Make sure to put that contact as the first reference in your profile. For most of you, this will probably be your club team head coach. Also, keep in mind that college coaches will want to speak to your club coach rather than your high school coach regardless of who you put as a reference.

When completing this section, list the contact's full name first, followed by their email and cell phone number. This should be sufficient for any college coach.

Sample player profile

See below for an example of a player profile.

Joe Brown

Position: Center Forward

Height: 6'0"   **Weight**: 170 lbs.

Email: **JBrown@example.com**

Cell Phone: (XXX) XXX-XXXX

Academic Background

- Cumulative GPA: 3.79
- ACT: 31
- 20 hours of college credit accumulated

Club Soccer

- Captain, Atlanta United Academy USSDA 2019
- 2017 Region III Premier League (R3PL) Runner-up

- GA '95 Boys ODP Team 2015-17
- 2017 Region III '95 Boys ODP Pool
- 2x US Soccer Development Academy (USSDA) Participant
- 2013 National Super-Y ODP Camp
- 2014 & 2015 Disney Showcase Champion
- 2x Disney Showcase Semi-finalist
- <insert any links to articles here>

International Soccer

- Trained in with Boca Juniors Academy and played the youth academies of River Plate, San Lorenzo, and Vélez Sarsfield.
- Trained in London & Manchester (Manchester City and Fulham) for one week, playing against the youth academies of Aston Villa, Coventry City and Crystal Palace.

High School Soccer

- 2015 4A Quarterfinals
- 2015 Newcomer of the Year Award
- 2015 2nd Leading Scorer
- 2016 4A Playoffs
- 2016 Leading Scorer
- 2016 All-county Team
- 2016 First All-region Team
- 2016 Best Offensive Player Award
- 2016 Most Outstanding Player Award
- <insert any links to articles here>

References

- **John Doe** – Executive Director, Atlanta United Academy: (XXX) XXX-XXX, **johndoe@example.com**
- **David Whitney** – Head Coach, Fulton County High School: (XXX) XXX-XXX, **johndoe@example.com**
- **Hank Brown** – Head Coach, Atlanta United Academy: (XXX) XXX-XXX, **johndoe@example.com**

Film your matches

At this point in the process, filming your games is necessary to prepare for Phase 3. However, you could even start doing this as early as your freshman year. Make sure you prioritize filming your club games rather than your high school games. It's usually not difficult to find one parent from your club team to film most games in a season so just ask around if no one is doing it currently.

At the end of your club season, you need to have at least three entire games filmed. This will make more sense in the next chapter when we discuss your highlight tape as a part of your brand.

Execute the Phase 2 email strategy

Your email strategy for Phase 2 will consist of several waves of emails over the course of your club season. For some of you this will last the entire school year, but this will be carried out over either the fall or spring for many of you.

It's very common for teams to have a tournament or showcase that they will attend at the beginning of their regular season and at the end of their regular reason. If your season resembles this format, then the idea is to send one email per major segment or part of your season. That way, each email is logically coherent, does not contain too much information, and the total number of emails sent during your season is not excessive.

Specifically, continuing with the format described above, one email will be sent a week before your first showcase, one email will be sent a week before your regular season starts, and one email will be sent one week before your final showcase. Below these three emails are referred to as email #1, email #2, and email #3, respectively.

It is important for you to adjust the schedule and timing of these emails to the structure of your season. That is, the major segments of your season should be easily identifiable. Furthermore, three emails is the minimum you should do. For example, if your team participates in three showcases in addition to your regular season, then four emails would be appropriate. If your season stretches 10 months then you will want send more than three emails over that period.

One tip you should follow anytime you are emailing a coach is to send it as continuing the chain of previously exchanged emails. That way, the coach can easily look back at previous emails for context, and won't have to work hard to remember past conversations. See below for an example of this.

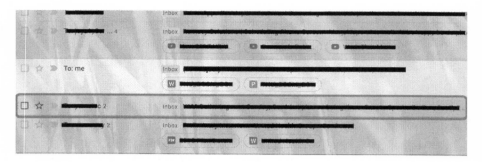

When doing this, you first need to find the chain of emails either under your inbox or sent mail (See red outline above). In the image above, you can tell if you are looking at an email chain if it has a number next to the sender. Once you find what you're looking for, click on that email chain.

After you've clicked on the chain, the last email in the chain should be in plain sight. Notice the reply icon in the top right above. Click the reply button to send another email to the recipient as a part of the email chain.

After clicking the reply button, you should be able to type your new email as normal. Once you're done, just click send as outlined above. Note that your email account may have a different layout or features but this should clarify the concept of continuing the email chain.

Phase 2 email #1 template

Coach (Insert Coach's Last Name),

Hope you're doing well. I'm writing in order to follow up from my first email. Below is a tournament that my team, *(Insert Name of Team)*, will be attending this *(Insert Name of Month)* before our season kicks off, and I have attached the schedule below for your convenience. We will also be participating in *(Insert Name of Tournament)* in addition to *(Insert Level of Regular Season Competition)*. However, I will send more details regarding these as we get closer to them. Additionally, please see a profile of my career attached for your reference.

(Insert Name of Competition) – (Insert Range of Dates)

Date	Time	Teams	Field

The address to the (Insert Name of Sporting Complex) is:

(Insert Address of Sporting Complex) *

Sincerely,

(Insert Your Name)

*Repeat this for every sporting complex listed above

Phase 2 email #2 template

This second email template will be quite similar but will focus on your team's regular season competition. Make sure you know where these games are posted online so you can send the coach the link to schedule.

It's better to send a link to the season schedule rather than a table within the email as in the previous example because the logistics of league games often change, whereas this is like less in tournament or showcase.

Coach (Insert Coach's Last Name),

Hope you're doing well. As mentioned in my previous email, Please see the link below for my *(Insert Level of Regular Season Competition)* regular season schedule. The games will take place in the following states *(List Names of States)*. We will also be participating in *(Insert Name of Tournament After the Regular Season)*, and I will send those details in another email. Additionally, I have attached an updated player profile. Please let me know if you have any questions about our season. Thanks

(Insert Schedule Link Here)

Best Regards,

(Insert Your Name)

Phase 2 email #3 template

This email template fundamentally accomplishes the same goals as the first two in the email strategy. However, you want to vary up your language and word choice as often as possible in order to seem like you didn't just copy your last email and just changed a few words.

Coach (Insert Coach's Last Name),

I trust that you're well. With our final showcase of the season coming up, I wanted to get you the schedule. Below is the schedule for my team, *(Insert Name of Team)*, for *(Insert Name of Tournament)*. Additionally, here is a link to the same schedule online:

(Insert Schedule Link Here).

Again, if you have any questions about the logistics of our showcase, please let me know.

(Insert Name of Competition) – (Insert Range of Dates)

Date	Time	Teams	Field

The address to the (Insert Name of Sporting Complex) is:

(Insert Address of Sporting Complex) *

Best,

(Insert Your Name)

Remember that these email templates are not designed to be rigid. Meaning, if your situation requires you to add some additional information that was not included in the template, go ahead and do it. The email templates you will find throughout this book are designed to be appropriate for the average recruit.

Finally, you want to send all the coaches on your list an email at the end of the year (If you play club soccer in the fall this will be after your high school season). In this email you should just provide a recap of your year. This may include a summary of your club and high school seasons and an unofficial transcript that details the courses you recently completed. Note that if you mention any attached documents in your email (such as the unofficial transcript mentioned below) then you need to actually attach them.

Coach (Insert Coach's Last Name),

I wanted to give you a quick recap of my accomplishments that took place during *(Insert Appropriate Period of Time)*. The following delineates my progress in *(Insert Appropriate Teams / Competitions)*:

> (Insert List of Accomplishments as a Bulleted List)

Additionally, please see my unofficial transcript attached after my sophomore year *(Or Other Appropriate Year)*.

Again, if you happen to play Development Academy, then you should just send this email at the end of your season when school is also finished.

Checklist before moving to Phase 3

At this point you've learned everything about initiating more consistent communication with coaches and developing a solid player profile. Make sure you've completed the following steps in Phase 2 before doing anything in Phase 3. Remember to go back and review specific sections as needed. Phase 2 is a crucial step because it sets the stage for Phase 3, which will be the phase in which you have the most contact with coaches. Make it your goal in this next phase to get the point where writing these emails and talking to coaches becomes second nature.

This moment should also be used to update your player profile with everything that happened over the year you just completed. In the above email, you just gave coaches a recap of your year. Make sure that summary is reflected on the player profile that you will attach to your future emails.

Phase 2 Checklist

- ✓ Send three emails to every school on your list during club season
- ✓ Have at least 3 entire games filmed
- ✓ Send final email in June/July to every school on list
- ✓ Update player profile after sophomore year
- ✓ Narrow down your list to 25 schools

Note that I have, again, added a task to this list. You have already narrowed down your list from 100 to 50 schools. At this point, you need to shorten the list to 25 schools. You should do this based on your interests, responses from coaches, continued research, personal reflection, your priorities, and intuition, which all may or may not have changed since the last time you whittled down your list!

Chapter 5:
Phase 3

Congratulations! You have now reached Phase 3, the most exciting and important part of the recruiting process. Most college coaches spend the majority of their allocated recruiting time pursuing players who are juniors in high school. Challenge yourself to focus even more now than you have in the previous two phases.

Read over your emails even more carefully, be precise and intentional in your speech when talking to college coaches, train extra hard, and prepare well for every game and never go through the motions. If you do these things, you could easily find yourself giving your verbal commitment before the year is out.

In this phase you'll record more of your matches, execute the phase 3 email strategy, start to talk with college coaches on the phone, and go on visits. Your brand should be fairly mature at this point in the recruiting process. After several waves of emails, coaches should have a pretty good idea of what you're all about as a person, student, and player.

Keep in mind that Phase 3 may spill over into the beginning of your last year of high school depending on your situation. It's not unusual for the majority of your visits to take place during the beginning of your last year. Don't compare yourself to others when they go on visits, get offers, and make verbal commitments. If you continue to focus on what you can control, then you give yourself the best possible change to succeed at collegiate level.

Criteria for proceeding

Again, make sure you have executed the phase 2 email strategy, filmed no less than three whole games, updated all coaches on your list at the end of the year, revised your player profile, and narrowed down your list to 25 schools before reading any further.

Make sure you take a second to review the checklist at the end of the last chapter in case you need a more thorough reminder regarding any of the phase 2 steps. If you have closely followed the steps outlined in Phases 1 and 2 thus far, then you are well on your way to ultimate success in the recruiting process.

Understand the importance of phase 3

Take a moment to reflect on the importance of this period in the grand scheme of the recruiting process. The time you have now is absolutely invaluable. Some prospects will start to see the fruit of their labors and stop working hard at this point in the process just as momentum is picking up. However, this is the time to focus your energy on what's important. You can do it.

Make a highlight tape

You will now make your first highlight tape, an essential part of your soccer brand. If you remember back to the previous chapter, you were instructed to film at least three of your club games during Phase 2. While three games are a good start, it's not enough footage to draw from in order to compose a good quality highlight tape. Simply put, the more film you have, the more you have to work with for a good highlight tape.

That being said, in this phase, you need to continue filming as many games as possible. At a minimum you should have footage from five additional games. That would get you to eight total games to draw your highlight tape from.

The purpose of creating a highlight tape in the first place is for college coaches to see a quick glimpse that will tell them what you are all about as a player (your brand). In your highlight tape you want to make sure you tailor it to position-specific skills, showcasing your greatest attributes. For example, if you are not a goal scorer, it wouldn't be smart to put every goal you scored between U10 and U17 in your highlight tape. That's not to say that you cannot include any goals in your tape, but you get the point.

Specific skills as mentioned above include things like passing ability, defending, dribbling ability, and finishing. These can even be broken down further. Here are a few examples:

- Passing ability

- o Driven balls
- o Passing over distance
- o Combination play
- Defending
  - o 1v1 defending
  - o Aerial challenges won
  - o Tackling
- Dribbling ability
  - o Skill in tight spaces
  - o Taking defenders 1v1
  - o Dribbling at pace
- Finishing ability
  - o Curling shots
  - o Striking from distance
  - o One-touch finishing
  - o 1v1 finishing

Keep in mind that the above list is not meant to be exhaustive so something else not listed here may be more appropriate for your position. You should definitely not utilize most of these categories/subcategories but rather pick three or four pertinent to your position and hone in on them.

For example, if you want to be recruited as a holding midfielder, you may choose to focus on passing over distance, positional defending, aerial challenges, and ability to make good decisions in possession for your highlight tape. If you're a defensive midfielder reading this, you may have different categories in mind that are more consistent with your game.

Many people out there will have differing opinions on how long a highlight tape should be. However, you need to keep it to around five or six minutes max. It needs to be around five minutes because, honestly, people start check out if it's too long. Besides that, remember that your highlight tape is supposed to be a glimpse of your ability, not a documentary. Somebody else will make your documentary if you play 10+ years at the highest professional levels. Capping out your highlight tape at five minutes also prevents you from including clips that don't really add any significant value to you brand. That is, when deciding what to include and what not to include in your tape, always ask "How does this contribute positively to my soccer brand?".

You might be wondering how you will put together a good quality highlight tape once you obtain the film. Good news is that you have many free options. Here are just a few:

- iMovie (Mac)
- Blender (Windows and Mac)
- Shotcut (Windows and Mac)

If you have a Mac, any of the three are fine; however, iMovie comes preinstalled on every Mac and it's pretty intuitive to use. Blender and Shotcut are also good options but you should definitely do your own research and experiment with different programs before you start editing your highlight tape. I personally have only used iMovie but wanted to provide you with other options for your highlight tape.

Furthermore, the highlight tape you send to coaches should not be overly flashy. Dramatic sounds effects or music should be kept out completely. If you're insistent on including some type of music pick a good instrumental (i.e. 300 Violin Orchestra). Other appropriate video effects include an introduction title, spotlights on you before the clip begins, and simple transitions between clips. An alternative to the spotlight would be an arrow that identifies you. While all of the above are beneficial they certainly aren't deal breakers for a highlight tape. A simple string of clips is sufficient and better than nothing. It's very easy to say that you'll make your highlight tape later. Do this work early on and you'll have a fantastic tool to showcase your soccer brand for the rest of the recruiting process.

Once you have your highlight tape as a .mp4 or .mov file you need to create a Google account/YouTube channel and then post your highlight tape to YouTube. Making a Google account and YouTube channel is completely free and easy to do. As you are uploading, you should either make your highlight tape public or unlisted. A public video is just as it sounds. Any normal video you would watch on YouTube is public. An unlisted video is only viewable to those who possess the video's link. When you publish as unlisted, you will be provided the URL, which you can easily share with college coaches in an email. It doesn't really matter which option you choose, rather, it just depends on what you'd prefer.

The most important thing to remember when constructing the highlight tape is to not include anything inconsistent with your soccer brand. When you include footage that is inconsistent with your soccer brand you confuse coaches. Before you start creating your highlight tape, I'd recommend rereading Chapter 1's Introduction – specifically the part about your soccer brand.

Gather footage of an entire match

Along with your highlight tape, you need to gather footage of an entire game on film. This is aspect of Phase 3 is the perfect complement to your highlight tape for building an effective soccer brand.

Having an entire game on tape allows college coaches to see your tendencies, thought processes, a run of decisions, positional play, and leadership abilities. It is these sorts of characteristics that are difficult for a highlight tape to capture. A college coach can see your thought processes during periods of the game where the pace of play is high, for example. College coaches will want to know if you can process issues on the field quickly and effectively. A great example of a series of decisions a coach would want to see would be transitional plays in the game. That is, once you win the ball in midfield, do you look to play a quick combination and immediately release a winger for a counterattack? Do you follow up a good tackle with a blocked shot? Coaches will want to see a series of good decisions that stamp your influence on the match.

An entire game is also great at showcasing positional play. College coaches can see how plays develop and how you react and adjust your position to win that individual battle, to make that defense-splitting pass, to clear the ball off your own goal-line, or to score the game wining goal. Additionally, college coaches will look for leadership abilities in your filmed match. You could be pointing and directing traffic on the field or you could be encouraging your teammate after he/she made a good decision. Just as businesses can never have enough employees who are leaders, a team can never have enough leaders in the locker room, and college soccer is no different.

At this point you are probably wondering which match you should pick to complement your highlight tape. You might want to choose the match with your most spectacular moment on film; however, consistency matters so much the higher levels of the game. Instead, choose the match where you most consistently made the right decisions. Inconsistent players frustrate college coaches and one bad mistake is more likely to be punished at the college level than at the club level. If possible, you should pick a match from this year, as it will come off as more relevant to coaches. Furthermore, you shouldn't worry too much about this selection. While college coaches will certainly analyze your mistakes to some degree, they ultimately want to assess what you do well against the college standard. In short, don't feel like you have to pick the perfect game.

Finally, you need to post this entire game to your YouTube channel. Again this video can be public or unlisted, whichever you prefer. This is just so that college coaches will be able to conveniently view both your highlight tape and game footage.

Execute the Phase 3 email strategy

Like in Phase 2, the Phase 3 email strategy will consistent of several waves of emails over the length of your club season. The idea is to again send one email per major part of your season (i.e. showcase, beginning of the season, etc.). You can leverage the same templates provided in Phase 2; however, I'd encourage you to start writing all your emails from scratch now that you have some experience doing it. Doing this will raise your communication skills to the next level. Make sure you have your season mapped out clearly in your head so that you can use it as guide to time your emails strategically.

Remember that one email per segment of your season is the minimum you should do. These emails are ultimately conversation starters. For example, one of these emails might lead to a coach asking you to get him a piece of information that you don't have handy. When you get back to him it probably won't fit nicely in a particular segment of your season, and that's OK. Be flexible a practice your situational awareness skills throughout the recruiting process rather than being too rigid. Be flexible within reason instead.

Talk with coaches on the phone

During Phase 3, college coaches will be allowed to call you directly instead of you only being allowed to call them (this rule is set by the NCAA and is subject to change). The first thing you must do before you have your first call with a college coach is to understand the place of phone calls with college coaches in the recruiting process. Phone calls with college coaches should be valued more than exchanging emails with them. Calls are more personal and they will give both of you a better sense of each other.

Additionally, coaches will always remember their calls with players more than they will remember exchanging a few emails. The more confident and comfortable you are talking to coaches on the phone, the more you will stand out from the crowd. At this point in the recruiting process, email should primarily be used to set up calls with college coaches. Keep in mind that US colleges could be in one of four time zones so you need to specify EST, CST, MST, or PST. Sending coaches a calendar invite via your email would be ideal, as it will conveniently allow coaches to place it on their calendar while solving the potential issue of different time zones.

Now, most players will likely be pretty nervous the first time they get on the phone with a coach. That's completely normal. However, players need to realize that they will never get comfortable talking with college coaches on the phone or in person if they never start.

Depending on the schools on your list, you may be talking to the assistant coach or the head coach. Larger Division I programs usually delegate a large part of the recruiting work to assistant coaches while the head coach does most of the recruiting work for some smaller Division I schools and the other divisions. If you start talking with the assistant coach initially, you will want to talk to the head coach eventually as the head coach ultimately makes lineup, game-time, and big-picture decisions for their program.

Now that you understand the basics about talking with coaches on the phone, you need to have a game plan for the questions you will ask them (and coaches will expect you to have questions). Below you will see a list of questions that you could ask coaches; however, you need to always be aware of where you are at in the process with the particular school that you are communicating with. For example, you wouldn't ask, "How much of tuition does my scholarship cover" if it is only the first time you're speaking to the coach. If you are unsure whether a particular question is appropriate given the situation, ask someone you trust who has experience in college soccer recruiting. The next best person to ask would be your club coach. While you are on the phone with coaches, write down any questions of this kind. This will give you the chance to determine if they are appropriate or not and then ask them again at a later date if needed.

The answers to some of the following questions will be more important to you than those of others so it might be helpful to highlight these as a reminder.

Athletic Questions

What's your team culture like?

A coach should have complete clarity on kind of team culture the program aspires to achieve. See Chapter 7 for more on team culture and college soccer.

Where on the field could you seeing me playing for your program? What specific need could you see me fulfilling for your program?

This simple question allows you to see if you and the coach are on the same page when it comes to position.

How many incoming player redshirt on average? How likely would it be for me to be redshirted my first year?

This is important to know and often depends on your position. For example, goalkeepers usually redshirt their first year. Coaches usually have a process for how they use redshirts and you want to figure that out.

What is a typical week of training and games during the season?

This helps you visualize the life of a college soccer player in season.

What's a typical week look like out of season?

This helps you visualize the life of a college soccer player out of season.

Tell me about your coaching style?

Compare their answer to this question with your past experiences with coaches. You know those coaching attributes that connect with you most and those that don't.

Tell me about the team's playing style and your playing philosophy?

This helps you determine if the program's philosophy is consistent with your own.

How many other prospective student–athletes are you recruiting at my position?

The coach may already have other players committed for you position. This and the current roster should give you a rough idea of the competition for the starting eleven and playing time.

Academic Questions

What is the typical GPA of the team during an the school year?

The answer to this question tells you how committed the coach and players are to their studies. Think about how this affects players' attitude and the environment of the program.

How is the department (for my major) rated?

Before asking this question, do some research beforehand. You will most likely not learn a lot more about this from the coach directly but it is still a good question to ask.

What percentage of your players graduate in 4 years?

Note that this might be 2 years if you are looking at junior college programs.

Are there any specific academic team policies?

This shows you what standards the coach imposes beyond the field.

Are there any academic support programs in place specifically for student-athletes?

Many universities will have tutoring services and facilities set aside specifically for the academic success of student athletes.

How many (credit) hours do you tell your players to take during the season?

Some coaches feel very strongly about their players taking a lighter academic load during the season. Consider your major and how many college credits you come in with along with this to see how it might affect graduation. If you're unsure about this, work with a potential academic advisor.

How many hours do you tell your players to take out of season?

The answer to the last question will inform the answer to this one.

How do you handle situations where class conflicts with training?

The answer to this question depends on NCAA rules as well as if we are talking about missing training in season vs. out of season.

Is there the opportunity for players to get summer classes financed by the university?

Some universities and programs will provide some of the finances to incentivize their student-athletes to stay and/or take summer classes.

Campus Life Questions

Describe a normal day for one of your players.

Helps you understand players' morning routines, class schedule, practice times, meals, etc.

Describe the dorms that the freshmen typically live in during their first year.

Ask about their proximity to classes and athletic facilities as well.

Are students allowed to live off-campus?

Follow up question: Do most of your players live on or off campus?

Financial Questions

What is your process for renewing athletic money?

Each coach does this a little bit different so the answer is important if you expect to receive athletic aid.

What is the process for renewing my academic money?

Coaches will likely refer you to an academic representative to answer this question but coaches will like that you are thinking about academic aid as an equal opportunity to athletic aid.

Are any of your players employed during the year? If so, when are they employed and what kind of jobs are they eligible to do?

Some programs have many players that are employed at different times in the year while other programs have almost no players employed during the semesters. Coaches can play a role in encouraging or discouraging this.

What can and what cannot be covered by academic and athletic money?

This usually is never an issue but you want to be aware of any university rules when it comes to scholarships.

Are there any rules surrounding the total amount of athletic and academic money received?

Sometimes these rules can come into play for student-athletes who are exceptional on the field and in the classroom.

Will I still continue to receive my scholarship in the event of a career-ending injury?

This question is appropriate when an athletic scholarship has already been offered. This question might be used to decide between two options that have drastically different weights for academic and athletic scholarships.

Say I was to get a serious injury. What is the athletic department's policy regarding medical payments?

While most programs will take complete care of you if your injury happened as a result of participating in practice or games, you should still know the rules.

Remember that it's OK to ask a question via email as well. If you forget to ask a particular question at the end of a conversation you can tell this to the coach in an email and then ask your question.

Go on visits

Visits are central to the college recruiting process. They are one of the aspects of recruiting that players get most excited about; however, it's important to keep a level head when visits start to roll around.

Now, keep in mind that visits can be official or unofficial. It is better to do unofficial visits at local schools that are on your list because they will be much cheaper than if you were to take an unofficial visit out of state. Additionally, invitations to official visits might come later on in Phase 3 or the beginning of Phase 4 so it might be beneficial to knock out the local visits first. If an in-state school continues to be one of your top options then you can always consider taking an official visit there later on in addition to your unofficial visit.

Another benefit of doing this is that when you talk to coaches on the phone, you can tell them that you've already been on visits with other schools. You don't want to bring this up out of context, however. Many college coaches will ask you this out right or ask you where you're at in the recruiting process. At that time, it's appropriate to talk about visits at other schools with a coach. This immediately increases your perceived value in their mind since they probably know and respect the coaches at the other schools you've visited.

It's essential to take some time to prepare for a visit and then reflect on it afterwards. Before going on a visit, gather specific questions that you didn't get answered via phone or email, know your current priorities for the recruiting process so that you can assess the school with clarity, and make a mental note of your intuition during the visit. Do you feel at peace when visiting the school? Do you feel uneasy?

Lastly, understand that visits lead to offers! A visit is usually one of the last steps before a college offers you a spot in their program. If you have several visits scheduled (especially official visits), this is a great sign that the recruiting process is coming to a head. An invitation for an official visit shows that a coach is serious about you because he's willing to put skin in the game to get you on campus.

Checklist before moving to Phase 4

At this point you have taken the most important steps to achieving your goal of playing at the collegiate level. You have obtained a new perspective on your soccer brand through your highlight tape. You have strategically spent time on the phone with coaches and you have gone on both unofficial and official visits.

You should take the time to update your player profile with any new information that occurred during Phase 3. Make sure that you are continuing to attach your player profile to emails where appropriate. For example, you should not reattach your profile for every short reply to a quick email. Rather, it is best to attach it when checking in after a while or prior to a visit. However, these should be fewer and farther between as your communication increases with only a handful of schools.

Phase 3 Checklist

- ✓ Make and upload your highlight tape
- ✓ Gather and upload footage of one entire match
- ✓ Execute Phase 3 email strategy
- ✓ Talk to coaches on the phone and get your questions answered
- ✓ Go on unofficial and official visits
- ✓ Narrow down your list to 5 schools

Congratulations on getting to this point. Continue to work just as hard as you did in the beginning, as you are now closer than ever before to playing college soccer. Finishing strong cannot be understated. You still have the most important decisions to make in the next phase.

Chapter 6:
Phase 4

You have now completed the most critical period in college soccer recruiting. However, you have not achieved your goal yet. You may even have several offers at this point. Phase 4 will continue to push you to finish strong regardless of how far along you think you are.

Finally, take one more moment to update your player profile one last time. Again, make sure to add any significant athletic and academic accomplishments, team changes, height/weight changes, and things of that nature. An updated photo would also be a good idea at this point. However, whatever you decide you want this photo to make it consistent across your player profile, email headshot, and email signature.

Criteria for proceeding

Make sure you have made and uploaded your highlight tape, uploaded an entire match, executed the phase 3 email strategy, spoken to college coaches on the phone, taken unofficial and official visits and narrowed down your list to 5 schools before continuing this chapter. Phase 3 is a critical time in the recruiting process so make sure to do your due diligence. You are closer to achieving your goal than ever before!

Additionally, if you are approaching the end of your high school career and have not checked off some of the phase 3 items, don't lose hope. This is the situation for many prospects just starting their senior that are very talented but are behind in the recruiting process. They haven't fully developed a player profile, they may not have their narrowed list, and they may not have a highlight tape but it's never too late to make a new beginning. Many great players don't commit until their senior year and if you get serious now, you can absolutely use the concepts in this book to get where you want to go in the game.

Achieve your goal and manage your time

At this time, I want you to take a moment and think back to the goal you set in the beginning of the recruiting process during Phase 1. Remember WHY you started in the first place. Think about this and remember the deadline you set to achieve your goal by. Honestly assess where you are at and then recommit to your goal. This moment is not about beating yourself up if you're not exactly where you would like. This moment is about gearing up one last time to get across the finish line for those of you who have not achieved your goal yet.

For those of you who have achieved your goal, remember that you are not finished yet! The choices you make on and off the field after you commit are just as important as those that got you to this point. Your goal should reach beyond getting to college soccer – you should be striving to be successful once you get there. Now that you've got there, prepare to succeed there.

It's easy to become unfocused academically and athletically after you commit and I've seen so many players do this. I encourage you to fight this temptation. If you successfully push through those final few months, you will be so glad that you did once you arrive on campus. One of the best things you can do during this period is to find someone to train with or train you. When setting out to do anything meaningful, doing it with others helps you be accountable, develops a sense of something larger than yourself, and makes it more enjoyable.

Items you need to know before you commit

So, you think you are ready to make your decision? Make sure you can answer the following before you commit to a program.

How much will you play?

This question is obviously impossible to answer with a high level of certainty; however, you want to get an idea of what's in the coach's head. Pay very close attention to coach's tone and word choice during your discussions about playing time. How does this tone and word choice compare to when he talks about current starters or other recruits coming in? While I wouldn't suggest putting the entire weight of your decision on this aspect, it's something you should definitely observe.

What position are you coming in to strengthen?

Notice that I said position and not positions. What singular need is the coach bringing you in to fill? This is not to say that you can't play other positions; however, if the coach routinely talks about you filling one of four positions on the field then you might want to take a closer look at the coach's intentions for you. On the other hand, it is a great sign when the coach frequently talks about you filling a specific need. Again while this is not a deal breaker, it's something you should always have in the back of your head when you are speaking with college coaches. If this is not a topic that has come up, you need to bring it up to coach immediately and get his feedback.

What will be expected of you performance-wise during your time there?

The answer to this question relates to the answer of the previous question. For example, if you're coming in to become the program's out and out forward eventually then the coach will have an expectation of how many goals per season you will score. If you're a center back, will you be the center back that others look to for strong leadership? Sometimes coaches will state this more explicitly and sometimes it will come more subtly.

This is important because you want to square up the coach's expectations with how you view yourself as player. For example, say you see yourself as a creative number 10 who can chip in with goals on the occasion. However, your focus is on playmaking in the final third. If a coach wants you to almost play as second forward and contribute with 7 or more goals per season then that program might not be the best fit for you. Keep this in mind as well as you get a feel for the previous question.

What is the Deadline of the offer?

Every offer has a deadline. Coaches want to make sure they don't miss out on other good players should you choose to not join their program. It's important to know where you stand with all schools and the deadlines for each school's offer if applicable. Ideally, you would like to start receiving offers at the same time but, in reality, this is almost never the case.

In my own experience, this highly influenced the timing of the decision. I had offers from three schools that came in all around the same time. However, I was still talking almost daily to three additional schools that had not offered me yet. When the subject of a deadline came up, I suggested the same date to all three coaches and they agreed that it was a reasonable date. Should I have let my deadline expire in the hope of more future offers? Not necessarily. It ultimately depends on what your goal is, what you want, and what schools you currently have offers from. Do your current offers serve your goals? If they're not even close then you should tell the coach that you're not interested so no one's time is wasted. If you're on a fence about this question then take the period to seriously reflect on your goals as well as what you have on the table. Above all though, never make a decision motivated by fear or scarcity. And never let a college coach put an unreasonable amount of pressure on you to make a decision. You've owned the recruiting process for yourself up to this point. Don't change your philosophy just because an offer is on the table.

What is your total scholarship per year precisely?

This includes academics, soccer, and any other scholarships you might receive. Again, you need to know this number precisely and not approximately. Finances are a key component of your decision. Take the time to crunch the numbers and ask your coach if there is any ambiguity. You should never be embarrassed to ask for clarifications on an important decision.

Once you have this number, you will know how much you will have to pay out of pocket to attend that school. Many players will ignore this aspect of the decision and pretend like it does not exist. They will do anything to justify paying any amount if they really want to attend that school. Keep in mind that the financial consequences of your college decision (whether you are going as an athlete or not) will last much longer than four years. This is true in both the negative and positive sense. A good return on investment for your education will pay dividends the rest of your life. Similarly, student loans have the ability to also follow you for the rest of your life. Regardless of what you decide it's essential to educate yourself thoroughly.

Commit to a school

You now possess everything you need to know before making your commitment. If at this time you are unsure about anything about developing your soccer brand or a specific step in the process go back and reread that section.

Go back to when you discovered what you wanted in a school. At that time, I took you through rigorous screening criteria for the schools you put on your list. Go back and make sure that the schools currently offering you still meet those criteria. This is very important.

Secondly, don't discount your intuition. Did you get an encouraging and positive vibe from the coach when you were on campus? Did your relationship grow with the coach during each phone call? Did you feel at peace when exploring the program? These are the sorts of experiences that shape your intuition, which ultimately influences your decision. Having a healthy reflection on both the rationale of your decision as well as your feelings will produce the best possible result.

Take care of your body

The most fundamental characteristic a player can have is availability. Take care of your body in these last few months to make sure you are available when the college season rolls around.

Minimize your chance of injury

Avoiding all chance of injury is impossible. However, you will minimize your chance of getting injured prior to your college season if you do the following:

- Don't play in meaningless competitions

- Stretch daily
- Exercise to maintain strength, stability, and balance

What do I mean by not playing in meaningless competitions? I'm talking about adult leagues, pick up, or any games that involve your family or buddies. Doing this is, honesty, just not smart. If you were to get injured during a pick up game right before your college season, you would certainly regret it. Furthermore, you are more likely to get injured in such a game than you are in one of your club games. This is a necessary sacrifice for any incoming college soccer player.

Secondly, develop a stretching routine and stick to it. Pick a particular time of time and be consistent (keep in mind that it's best to do static stretching after you train). Additionally, you should hold every stretch for about 20 seconds before moving on. Furthermore, target the parts of your body that are consistently tight and do multiple stretches/reps for those particular areas. Stretching something that's really easy to throw aside and not find time for, but I can tell you that you will feel healthiest when you have a consistent stretching routine.

Lastly, you must exercise to maintain your strength, stability, and balance. Notice that I said "maintain" and not "increase". Being sharp in the fundamentals of the game and your fitness should be your top priorities the closer you get to preseason; however, adding some exercises to your summer program for the maintenance of your body will decrease your chance of injury significantly.

Eat well

This is not intended to be a crash course in nutrition; however, eating well does reduce you're chance of injury because it gives your body the fuel to do what it needs do on the pitch. Focus on changing one thing at a time as well. For example, first you could cut out all junk food immediately. That is, candy, cake, or anything with refined sugar is no longer on your menu. I just want to make you more conscious of what you're fueling your body with for competition rather than giving you an exact plan.

What training should you be doing during this period? Most of this work will take the form of training you do on your own. I believe that individual training is irreplaceable regardless of age or level simply because you touch the ball so many times in a short period of time. This training is time you set aside specifically to keep yourself sharp on the ball. I will touch on attaining a standard of fitness for preseason in a subsequent section.

This work that you do by yourself in the months leading up to your first college season will pay you dividends in a few short months. You will come in sharper and more focused than your teammates. Additionally, this will make up for any lack of athleticism you might have as a freshman. If you're already an outstanding athlete as a freshman at the college level, the technical training you do will complement your God-given gifts unlike anything else you do.

Set a goal for your freshman year

It's proper that we start to set a new goal as we celebrate your accomplishment. I want you to set a goal for what kind of athletic impact you want to make during your first year. Go back and review the details of what comprises a **SMARTER** goal back in Chapter 1. As a quick reminder SMARTER [2.] stands for:

- **S**pecific
- **M**easurable
- **A**ctionable
- **R**isky
- **T**ime-keyed
- **E**xciting
- **R**elevant

For example, the goal of a center forward could be to start at least 75% of games and score at least 7 goals during freshman season.

This is goal is specific. It is clearly measurable, time-keyed, relevant and exciting but it's also risky too. The goal is ambitious and will require a lot of sacrifice to achieve. Since it's ambitious it will be difficult to achieve. This is the sense in which these types of goals are "risky".

Your head coach will want to see you play again

After your commitment, your head coach will absolutely want to see you play at least once more before you arrive on campus. This will somewhat factor into his plans for you once you arrive on campus because it's the most recent image he will have of you as player until he gets you in the program. The coach just wants to see how you are progressing. The same is true of anyone who makes an initial investment in anything. If you invest in a particular fund many people will want to check back in at point to see how their investment is doing. Your college coach may have already invested some athletic money in you at this point and he wants to know that you are progressing toward the college standard.

Keep this in mind and you will be motivated to keep pushing yourself during this crucial period. Some players relax and change their attitude once they've committed; however, this is the time to increase your commitment and work hard. When you've been working hard on the field and trying to attain your aspirations of playing collegiately for so long it can be temping to just take a few months off. However, I promise you that you will be very happy that you continued training and pushing yourself once you arrive on campus.

Sign your letter

Before signing day rolls around you need be somewhat prepared for the events that will take place. As I stated at the beginning, this book is not intended to be the recruiting gospel for keeping NCAA compliance. However, I do want to emphasize that you need to learn about signing day before it happens. Your head coach will usually give you an overview of what needs to happen and when. If you have any confusion at all about signing day you need to reach out to your compliance officer and definitely copy your coach in on the email. It would also be beneficial to talk to someone who has gone through signing day before. The big thing is to just make sure everything in the letter looks correct and know what you are responsible for doing.

Graduate high school

Graduating high school may sound like a given for most prospects but make sure to finish strong academically. Know that any of your academic scholarships will likely hinge on you finishing with a certain GPA amongst other criteria. If you don't have any academic scholarships then you will also want to finish strong because every college and university has minimum standards for acceptance. Schools usually accept you conditionally and assume that you will have approximately the same GPA when you graduate. You always hear stories of specific in high school player that never got the opportunity to continuing playing at the next level because he didn't take care of things in the classroom. I'm sure you can think of at least one person who fits that narrative.

This aspect of the recruiting process is almost 100% controllable. If you have made it this far in your educational career you can graduate high school. Knowing that college soccer is in your future should motivate you to finish what you started both athletically and academically.

Stick to your conditioning program

It is standard for every college program to have at least a summer running program in preparation for preseason. Additionally, it's not uncommon for this to be supplemented with a bit of weights or body weight exercises. You need to stick to this program. You need to arrive at preseason fit rather than using preseason to get fit. The goal is to build your fitness up gradually until the point of preseason.

Many players (especially freshman) come in not at full fitness and get injured during preseason. If you build your way up to maximum fitness over the summer then you will give yourself a great chance to have an injury-free start to the season.

If the only program they give you involves running then you could add some body weight exercises with the running in order to maintain your strength. Focus especially on exercises that build core strength. A strong core will vastly benefit your performance as everything in soccer requires core strength.

Chapter 7:
Other Items to be Aware of

Adapting the process for the women's game

As I touched on in Chapter 2, the timeline presented in this book can easily be modified to fit individuals in their particular situation. While I don't want to go into detail about the timeline for women because I'm simply not as familiar with it, the main aspect you need to realize is that sophomore year is the big year for recruitment in the women's game.

Consequently, shifting everything earlier can solve most discrepancies regarding timing. Furthermore, Phase 1 and 2 will become more condensed to a certain degree in order to prepare for a successful Phase 3.

Additionally, the purpose of this book is to teach you how to navigate the college recruiting process. That is, I want you to understand the concepts and nature of college recruiting. This (along with some self-awareness) is the most important attribute you need to be successful in the college soccer recruiting process. Again, if you're getting caught up in the timing of things then you're missing the point of the recruiting process in the first place. You will forget everything about building your soccer brand when you are wasting time worrying about a milestone that you haven't hit in the recruiting process.

Adapting the process for different club and high school seasons

Some players reading this book will be playing with their club teams in different competitions year round. However, some of you may be playing with your club teams half the year and spending the other half in high school soccer. Since the structure of youth soccer in the United States currently offers several different paths, I wanted to address this briefly. My intention is not to evaluate the different programs out there but rather to help all players adapt the process outlined in the previous chapters regardless of their playing situation. This is why I chose to refer to the components of the process as phases rather than "Year 3" or "Junior Year". Every player is unique and starts from a different place.

The one thing that will significantly change the timing of the different steps is high school soccer. Depending on what state you live in, high school soccer can either be played during the fall or the spring. Consequently, many club programs choose to start and finish in the opposite season. Because college coaches primarily care about your club career, I teach players to strategically communicate with coaches before and after their major tournaments and showcases. If you play club and high school soccer, you can easily shift the outlined email strategies to the part of the year when you are playing club soccer. Most of your emails during your club season should be focused on providing coaches your game schedule. On the other hand, most of time during the high school season should be spent updating coaches on what you are doing, enhancing your player profile, developing your highlight tape, getting coaches on the phone, and things of that nature. Approaching tasks this way will lay the groundwork for the following season.

Finally, realize that the landscape of youth soccer is changing so rapidly in the United States that focusing on the concepts of the steps in the different phases is much more important than the timing of things. When the focus is developing your brand to present to college coaches there is always something you can be doing regardless of the season or time of year.

DI, DII, DIII, NAIA, NJCAA, and NCCAA Soccer, Their Similarities, and Differences

In this section the differences in athletics and school experience will be discussed rather than focusing on the differing bylaws that govern each division. For a more in depth discussion on rules specific to a division, you should reach out to school compliance officers.

Before discussing the specific differences between the different divisions, you should know that it is in your best interest to not limit yourself to only considering schools in one division. Many prospects have the attitude that they must play DI for one or more of the following reasons:

- I have aspirations to play professionally
- Any other division is below my level
- I want to go to a big school
- I want to play in a particular conference (i.e. ACC)
- All my teammates are going DI

Instead of hitting of the above individually, I will explore the most prevalent beliefs. DI does not exponentially increase your chances of making it to the professional ranks. Chris Wondolowski is among the best examples to look to. Chico State coach "Mike O'Malley noticed Wondolowski at a tournament late in his high school career. O'Malley invited him to check out the school, and extended Wondolowski his only scholarship offer for soccer." [3.] . Yes, Wondolowski, the all-time leading scorer in Major League Soccer was only offered an athletic scholarship by one school. Also, notice how late he was picked up in high school (during Phase 4). If Wondolowski had quit due to the lack of interested coaches, then he never would have made it to Chico State. Chris went on to boast 39 goals and 23 assists in 84 games over his college career [3.]. "San Jose Earthquakes of Major League Soccer took a chance on Wondolowski by picking him in the league's supplemental draft." [3.]. Chris is now the all-time leading scorer in Major League Soccer history. You simply cannot dispute how ridiculously successful Wondo has been during his professional career in Major League Soccer without the interest of one even Division I coach.

Even if your goal is to play professionally, you still need to be realistic about the potential paths you can take to your goal. Another thing to consider is your chances of playing professionally vs. your abilities on another path. That is, the majority of kids going into college soccer would be better-suited taking academics at least as seriously as they take soccer. Athletic departments should want to prepare their student-athletes to be successful once they graduate just as much as they want to prepare them to perform on game days. They know as well as anyone that most of their student-athletes will not reach the professional ranks.

That being said, for the overwhelming majority of players, any division will not be below their level. Just because you dominate over a season or two doesn't necessarily mean the competition is below your level. How many players in professional soccer can dominate a game with one team and then struggle to adjust once they move on to a bigger club? Keep in mind that players have gone up to the professional ranks from every division in college soccer (even DIII).

There are some additional things you should understand about the different levels of college soccer. The difference in quality between Division 1 and Division 2 is not as big as you think. In fact, the only real difference is athleticism. That is, the average player in DI is significantly faster and stronger than that in DII. To my knowledge, this small difference between DI and DII is not present in most other collegiate sports, making college soccer recruiting a bit unique. For men's soccer, DII and NAIA are roughly comparable levels; however, NAIA seems to have more variability. This means that you will find fantastic teams at the top of NAIA as well as some teams that don't look like they belong at the bottom of NAIA. DIII is more or less its own animal. Again, the top teams in DIII could compete with most teams in any other division. Sometimes DIII schools will play less direct as athleticism isn't as much of a factor.

Division I

As discussed above, there are many attractive things about DI, but just because you have an offer from a DI school doesn't necessarily make it is the best choice for you. DI teams, on average will showcase the best level of competition college soccer has to offer. Perennial contenders such as University of Maryland, University of Akron, Clemson, and Stanford are all part of NCAA DI. The best conferences (in no particular order) for DI include the Atlantic Coastal Conference (ACC), Big Ten Conference (B1G), Pacific-12 Conference (Pac 12), and the Big East.

The DI game tends to be very physical, direct, and intense. Exceptional speed and strength are usually on display for any given match in DI. There are a fair minority of teams that try to put the ball on the ground while also still possessing that elite athleticism.

Pace of play is extraordinarily higher than that of youth soccer at the DI level. Players who process issues on the field the quickest tend to have more success. The physicality of games often breeds intensity and many fouls. However, this can also be said for college soccer as a whole to varying degrees.

Division II

Note that there will be different bylaws between DI and DII despite the fact that both are NCAA. For specific questions regarding differing bylaws contact the compliance officer or representative at the particular DII school you are interested in. While DII is also very physical, you do get teams playing a wide variety of styles. One reason for this could be that there are some teams with a disproportionate amount of foreign student-athletes. These players are sometimes from the same country and sometimes from different countries.

Overall, DII is a really interesting option that has a lot of attractive qualities. These include scholarship opportunities for fringe DI players, different types of schools with different feels, and fewer layers to the head coach to name a few.

When I was playing DII, there existed a "tryout rule" where high school players or transfers could come and practice with the team. I learned this during my time at Trevecca Nazarene University as we had many prospects come and try out. In fact, many of my teammates were offered a spot on the team as a result of their try out. While I'm sure many DII coaches do not make use this rule, it's these sort of things that are nice know when it comes to the division and/or coach.

Division III

DIII schools also have different NCAA bylaws when compared to those of DI and DII. Again, if you are looking into schools in different divisions you need to ask the head coach of those programs to get you in contact with their compliance officer for divisions specific compliance questions. For example, DIII schools cannot give athletic scholarships. Imagine the player who was banking on an athletic scholarship at DIII to get him/her through college. How sorry would this player be since they didn't ask about the rules before investing too much and having to backtrack? While this is an unlikely and extreme example it shows that if you have a compliance-related question you should write it down and ask!

If you're outstanding academically, you will want to consider some DIII schools in addition to DI schools since the best academic institutions belong to DI and DIII. There are also a handful of really good institutions at the DII level so I'd encourage you to do some research on those as well. For example, University of California San Diego (UCSD) is a fairly prestigious school but competes in DII. Be proactive and seek out unique schools like UCSD if they fit you. Remember that you will only ultimately only choose one school!

Furthermore, some DIII programs play at an exceptional level. Again, don't just assume DIII teams can't compete at the level of many DI teams. For example, Messiah College Men's Soccer won 10 National Championships in 14-year span [4]. One of their players several years back summed up their program well when he said, "We just want to be one of the best places in the country to play soccer" [4]. And he does not mean just in DIII. "Coach Brad McCarty estimates about half of his players could compete at the Division I level. They have the skill and technique to play at much bigger schools, but opt for the smaller-school experience for all kinds of different reasons" [4]. Hockensmith also emphasizes that Coach McCarty process of vetting players that are a good fit is a huge reason for their success [4]. College soccer coaches want to know that you are a good fit for their program just as much if not more than you want to find a school that's a great fit.

Telling you about Messiah Men's Soccer is the best thing I can do that to help you realize why you should consider schools in multiple divisions. As someone who played both DI and DII, I can tell you that the experience is different and only you can decide what you want out of your four years.

NAIA

The National Association of Intercollegiate Athletics (NAIA) is a completely separate governing body from the NCAA. For men's soccer the NAIA level is roughly comparable to Division II. However, there are some NAIA schools that are way off the Division II level and there are some that easily exceed it. Additionally, there tends to be more foreign players in NAIA from my experience.

Since the NAIA is completely separate from the NCAA it will have different regulations and rules that govern athletes. If you considering both NAIA and NCAA schools it is critical that you get both sets of rules clear in your head. Again, use compliance officers as resources as much as possible.

NJCAA

The National Junior College Athletic Association (NJCAA) is governing athletic body for junior college sports. Junior colleges take players into their programs for two years (where they often graduate with an associates degree) before they transfer to a four-year school to continue their career. Junior college is another great option that many players don't consider coming out of high school. You might choose the junior college route for one or more of the following reasons:

- A lack of finances to attend a four-year institution
- A lack of academic qualifications to attend a four-year institution
- A desire to continue living at home due to family obligations
- An interest to study a particular skill
- A need to continuing working while going to school and playing soccer

If any of the above resonated with you, I highly encourage you to check junior college programs in your immediate area, state, and across the country. Every year players from junior colleges transfer to all different types of schools. Many junior colleges athletes go on to be top players at the Division I level. The same can be said for just about every division except probably Division III. Considering the reasons above, a player wouldn't choose to transfer from junior college to DIII because DIII schools are usually private and therefore more expensive. Private DIII schools also tend to have higher academic standards, which is another reason players often choose junior college in the first place. I think you can see why most junior college players tend to choose DI, DII, and NAIA when transferring after two years.

Similarly to what was stated above in NAIA section, the NJCAA will have a separate set of rules when compared to the NCAA and NAIA. Make sure to keep this in mind throughout the recruiting process if you are considering NJCAA schools.

NCCAA

The National Christian College Athletic Association (NCCAA) is a completely separate competition relative to the NCAA, NAIA, and NJCAA. Only Christian schools can belong to the NCCAA. However, not all Christian schools actually belong to the NCCAA. Additionally, schools do not exclusively belong to the NCCAA. NCCAA competition can supplement a team's NAIA competition, for example.

You may be wondering what divisions NCCAA schools typically come from. The overwhelming majority of NCCAA schools come from DII. After that, NAIA probably has the best representation. Currently, NCCAA competition continues later in the semester (after most schools are done with their NCAA games). Since there are less total schools, it's quite common for a team to continue going deep in the NCCAA championship even if the team's NCAA competition has ended.

You also might be wondering why certain Christian schools prefer not to join the NCCAA. Take Messiah College Men's Soccer for example. Since Messiah is a perennial contender for the national championship, I'm sure they don't want to fill their season up with too many games.

Team culture

The first thing you must understand about the team culture of any sports team is that it is established from the head coach and then trickles down. This cannot be understated. If you like a coach's values beyond the soccer field, then there's a good chance you'll enjoy the team culture that coach stands by. Secondarily, the players a coach brings in always reinforce that same team culture and makes it likely to persist in the years to come.

For example, if coaches continually bring in players that genuinely care about their academics, then the team GPA should rise or continue to be very high. In such a team culture, the player who doesn't care about his/her academics is the odd one out. Moreover, his teammates will likely grill him about it on the occasion.

Just know that every program differs slightly in its team culture, and many times this is informed by the overarching culture of the university itself. For example, if the institution is religious then there is a good chance that the average student-athlete is more religious at that school than the average student-athlete at a public school. Other very select schools like Harvard have their own unique culture due to the type of students that come there every year, for instance. Do your own research into the culture of the university and the team by asking current players what their experience has been like.

While you are going through the recruiting process, try to glean as much information as possible regarding team culture. This will tell you something more personal about the coach and how it informs his recruiting philosophy and personal values. You may be tempted to gloss over this aspect of the process; however, it will turn out to be more important than you think.

International student-athletes

It's important that you realize that your competition for college soccer extends beyond the borders of the United States. That is, there are so many international prospects that would love to have the opportunity to come to America, study, earn a degree, and play soccer at a high level in the process.

Additionally, foreign student-athletes tend to receive more athletic aid than domestic players. This makes sense as foreign players incur more expenses and will generally have to give up more to leave their country. Because of this, college coaches have to offer a larger incentive for these players to make a big decision. It's the same as the job market. If an employer really wants a candidate from out of state to move to their city and work for them, wouldn't that employer offer moving assistance and other resources to make that transition easier? College soccer is like any other market where buyers and sellers come together. While international student-athletes generally receive more athletic scholarship this is not always the case. Don't just assume that because a player is foreign that he is automatically on more money than the next guy.

Another thing you need to know is that different coaches have different recruiting philosophies when it comes to bringing in international players. Some coaches draw heavily from their local area and the surrounding states while some draw heavily from different the international pool, and there are many coaches who fall somewhere in between. Even coaches on the extreme ends differ quite a bit. For example, one coach may recruit internationals exclusively from South America while another may recruit them exclusively from the United Kingdom. A good way to get a glimpse of the coach's view on this matter is to take a peek at the roster online that tells you where his players are from. You can count the number of foreign players relative to domestic players for the last several seasons. This will give you a better idea than just merely looking at the current year.

One example that sticks out in my head is Ohio Valley University (OVU) during my time in college. OVU averaged one to two American players on their roster during my time at Trevecca Nazarene University. The OVU program had a tremendous amount of success during that period as well. On the flipside, Messiah College primarily recruits from the American pool and has obviously had extraordinary success as well.

Coaches have been successful using all different types of international recruiting philosophies. All of the above should serve to inform you whether you are a domestic player or international player to help you make a fantastic choice for your collegiate career.

Club team recruiting brochures

One option that many clubs and teams don't consider as a practical option to increase exposure at showcases is recruiting brochures. A recruiting brochure provides basic information about the team, coach, and players. Ideally it would include team name, year, a few notable team accomplishments, the coach's email, the coach's phone number, player headshots, player emails, player phone numbers, player positions, player cumulative GPAs, and player SAT/ACT scores. Depending on your team and the showcase you're attending your team may find it beneficial to include some additional features or leave out some of the above.

Once your team has a brochure made you need to determine how many to bring to the showcase. Again, this will depend on the showcase. If you're going to one of the largest tournaments in the country (i.e. Disney Showcase, Dallas Cup, Surf Cup) then you could easily print out 100 brochures. For medium to small-sized tournaments your team should bring no less than 50 copies.

Finally, how should you go about getting these brochures into the hands of college coaches? First, you should give a handful of brochures to your team's head coach, as they will likely speak with college coaches at some point during the showcase. Team managers will likely have a fair number of copies; however, team managers should be cautious of approaching and talking to every coach they pass. Instead of first trying to speak to coaches, managers would probably be better off handing brochures to a coach and continuing on their way without saying a word. Lastly, if the facility has stadium seating then team managers can place brochures in the seats that college coaches usually occupy. One way to know where college coaches will be sitting and standing is for team managers to arrive at the facility beforehand and just watch where the coaches go.

Money and scholarships

I have already spoken some about scholarships in different places but I wanted to highlight a few points here:

- Focus on your total combined scholarship rather than just athletic money
- Know your number and don't compromise
- Make sure the timing is right when discussing athletic scholarships with coaches

- Do the math to estimate available scholarship money

Some players get hung up on feeling like they need some athletic aid to affirm them as a player. However, if you have the attitude that you are going to university for school and soccer then all you should really care about is your total scholarship amount. In fact, I would argue that the more academic money you have, the better. Think about it. If (God forbid) you were to have a career ending injury or a falling out with the coach then you could potentially lose your athletic scholarship. However, your academic scholarship is independent of anything that happens within the program. Your total number is all that matters once you become a student-athlete.

What do I mean by "Know your number"? I want you to know what you will and what you won't pay for college. If soccer were not in the picture, what would this number be for you? Take a second to think about that now. I want you to think about how you can use soccer to beat that number. Now, you may be thinking that you would not compromise a good college soccer experience to do this. This is a false dichotomy. I previously mentioned how players can often idealize a particular program or conference in their head as the pinnacle of college soccer. In this player's mind anything less is a compromise and will not produce a good college soccer experience. I know this is a false dichotomy because I've played in two very different college soccer programs and I know many other players who have done the same. Changing your mentality on this point will allow you to think "win-win" as opposed to thinking in a binary fashion. You can beat your number and have a fantastic college soccer experience. Lastly, don't compromise. Don't compromise because you can absolutely find a school that meets both your athletic and financial criteria.

I have stated previously that timing is everything when discussing athletic scholarships with coaches. If a player asks about athletic money too soon and too frequently then the coach will get the idea the player's decision is entirely dependent on this one factor. Consequently, that coach will probably think twice if that player is someone he wants to bring in the program. For this point, the biggest skill I can emphasize is self-awareness. Self-awareness will critical for any relationship and setting. Practice evaluating your level of self-awareness around your family and friends so that it becomes easy when you are visiting with college soccer coaches.

Additionally, make sure you do some basic math to get an idea of what the available scholarship money will be like up front. First off, this is a rough estimate and should be taken as gospel. There are two components to estimating the available athletic aid for a program at any given time. They are as follows:

- The number of graduating seniors
- The number of graduating seniors that are also international players

Once you know the above, you can assign 40% of a full scholarship to domestic graduating seniors who are starters and 80% of a full to international graduating seniors. Next, find the total estimated scholarship money for the senior class but adding up your values. Since coaches typically invest their entire outgoing scholarship money into their next class this number is a good estimate for the scholarships available for your incoming class. Let's do a quick example together:

Total number of graduating seniors: 8 (5 are starters)

3 of the 5 senior starters are international

$2*0.40 + 3*.80 = 3.20$ estimated full scholarships available

You may notice that our estimate is dependent on the accuracy of our 40% and 80% assumptions. Doing a sensitivity analysis can give a range for the estimate. For example, you could repeat the above exercise by using a range of inputs. 40% could range from 10% up to 60% and 80% could range from 50% to 100%. You can increment 10% by 5% up until you reach 60% to obtain your range. Repeating this for second input and applying the formula you will arrive at a high and low estimate for the total available scholarship for your class.

This may seem like a lot of work to do for every school just to get an estimate. I would recommend doing this just for your top schools as progress through the recruiting process. That way you generally know how much opportunity there is to receive a scholarship, as you are about to make your decision.

Chapter 8:
Frequently Asked Questions

What place do recruiting questionnaires have in the process?

There is nothing bad about recruiting questionnaires on university athletic websites; however, filling out excessive amounts of questionnaires is not the best use of your time. Instead, you should prioritize whatever item is most relevant in the particular phase you're in before moving on to submitting questionnaires.

One thing to understand about these questionnaires is that they are likely written for the majority of other sports and then modified for college soccer. For example, many questionnaires will go into detail about high school soccer and high school soccer accomplishments. Well, you don't have to be an expert on the recruiting process to know that college soccer coaches really could care less about your high school season. Rather, they all want to know about how you perform at the highest levels of club soccer.

From my personal experience, I probably only received no more than 15 emails from college coaches over the course of high school as a result of me filling out questionnaires for most of the schools on my initial list of 100 schools. And I spent a lot of time filling out questionnaires during my freshman and sophomore years.

In short, questionnaires can be used to supplement the plan; however, they should never become the focus of the process.

What place do college ID camps have in the process?

First and foremost, college ID camps are income-generating machines for most programs; however, that does not mean you can't have a good experience at them or that they cannot lead to a spot on a college team.

Specifically, these sorts of things really depend on the program. Some programs bring in one or more players from an ID camp every year while others draw virtually none of their roster from ID camps. If you have a connection with someone on the team, you should ask him how many current players came from the ID camp. This can even be a question you ask the coach if he asks you to attend one of his ID camps. If he can't demonstrate a history of bringing in players from the ID camp, it's probably not worth attending.

Just to give you a practical example, two of the players from my recruiting class at Ohio State were identified at the program's ID camp. There were others from the class prior to mine as well.

More than attending program exclusive ID camps for a particular university, I'd recommend attend camps through 3rd parties that have many colleges attending. These are often done through clubs or other organizations. Exact Sports is a great example of such camps. EXACT gives participants access to many other benefits while exposing them to dozens of colleges.

Again, rather than pouring money into multiple ID camps, you would be better off spending your time communicating with more coaches, guest playing in an additional showcase, doing a real tryout with a DII team, or attending a camp through a 3rd party.

What is my club coach's role in getting me to college soccer?

This is a great question because club coaches have the potential to play a massive role in the recruiting process. However, this typically depends on the strength and size of the coach's network with current college coaches. Some club coaches have extensive networks and talk fairly regularly with many college coaches while others may only know a few on a somewhat personal level. I would encourage you to discover what your club coach's network could potentially offer.

Furthermore, share your interests and where you're at in the process with your club coach. This will help him/her understand what you're looking for and ultimately help you achieve your goal. Once your coach knows what you're looking for, he/she can reach out to schools in his/her network that match your interests on your behalf. Make sure to have these sorts of conversations in a one-on-one setting and not in front of teammates or parents of teammates.

Keep in mind that the coaches you establish communication with will call your club coach eventually whether they know him or not. This will happen sometime during Phase 3 or 4. Make sure to stay up to date with your club coach on how their dialogue is going with different programs and what kind of feeling your club coach gets during their conversations. You want your club coach to be honest with you if he doesn't get a good vibe from a particular college coach, regardless of the relationship he may have with that college coach. Your club coach should not sacrifice his relationships with players for political gain in soccer.

In short, club coaches can provide tremendous opportunity for prospects to get to college soccer. However, not every player will know a coach personally with an wide-ranging network. This is why it's ultimately up to you to make things happen in the recruiting process.

How difficult is it to get a spot on a college soccer team?

I'll be completely honest with you. It's not easy. I won't lie. However, your continued effort and determination will immensely increase your chances of succeeding. If you follow the plan and heed the advice in this book about your attitude toward recruiting process then your chances are much better than the average youth player.

The best thing you can do when the process is difficult and you're feeling like you'll never make it to college soccer is to remember your why for starting in the first place. Remember your goal. These are the things that make the grind of the recruiting process is worth it!

How do I not come off as desperate when interacting with college coaches?

When interacting with college coaches, there a number of things you should focus on doing intentionally rather than spending time and energy worrying about appearing desperate. Keep in mind that the single most important thing you have when interacting with college coaches is complete clarity of who you are as a player and person. When you are single-minded regarding your identity it's very easy to exude confidence, which destroys any perception of desperation.

While many players think they have clarity about their soccer brand, they still struggle to communicate it to coaches effectively. You should practice a successful interaction with a college coach in your head. Speak it out loud even. Think about what kind of things appropriate to talk about given your familiarity with the coach, what stage you're at in the process, and what kind of signals the coach is giving off. Even before you start talking about anything substantial with a college coach, think about how you will break the ice. A great option is to break the ice by discussing what's happening at the moment in the professional game. Is the coach from another country? If so, he might be pleasantly surprised if you were to bring up the domestic league of that country in conversation.

When you eventually get in front college coaches make sure to speak smoothly and confidently. Clearly pronounce your words and don't ramble just to take up time. Be intentional with what you say. If college coaches can tell that you're not comfortable in your own skin around them, how confident will they be working with you once you actually arrive at their university?

Furthermore, if you know your value in the college soccer marketplace, why would you worry about what any one coach thinks about you? This usually stems from a player having a dream to play for a certain school or in a certain conference, and thinking anything less than that is a failure. While this is not necessarily a bad thing, you should focus more on if the coach and the program are a good fit, emotions aside. Additionally, sometimes what people think they want isn't actually what they want. A player might arrive at their dream school only to discover certain things about the program that were unknown previously because their emotions blinded them. Ultimately, authenticity will attract like-minded coaches to recruit you.

How do I manage having multiple offers while still talking with other schools?

Before you tackle this problem, take a second to reflect and appreciate how far you've come in the recruiting process. While working the process as described in this book tries to set things up for offers to come in at the same time, the reality is that they won't come in at exactly the same time. Therefore, it is not a matter of if you will have to deal with this, but rather when and how.

When making decisions surrounding the timing of offers, you should frame your thinking in terms of opportunity costs. Let me explain. Players will still have opportunity to receive more offers after the deadline of the first offer they receive. Furthermore, many players may be tempted to wait until a better offer comes along. The question you must ask yourself is the following:

"Is waiting for a potential better offer worth losing any current offer(s)?"

Additionally, know what a "better" offer would like to you. Does a better offer mean more scholarship? Does it mean a more prestigious academic program? Ultimately, only you can make this decision.

Above all, be completely transparent in your conversations with coaches who have offered you and who have not yet made you an offer. If you are very interested in a school that hasn't offered yet but are sitting on an offer, make the coach aware of the deadlines in front of you. Lots of times college coaches will be proactive and ask you if you've received any offers and will want to know your deadlines. Keep in mind that coaches talk to each other as well, which is another reason to be absolutely transparent.

What are some common mistakes players make when communicating with coaches?

Again, you should focus your energy on effectively communicating your personal soccer brand to college coaches. However, players who jump into the recruiting process unprepared often make the following mistakes:

"I'm looking to get a scholarship" [5.]

While this is not a bad personal goal it should never be stated like this to a college coach. This statement communicates to college coaches that you won't consider their program if they don't get a scholarship. It also communicates that's it's really the thing of penultimate importance in the recruiting process rather than the school being a good fit. It also diminishing your ability to build a relationship with the coach and hear him out when you just simply state that you're just looking for a scholarship.

While this is certainly the goal of every player, it can easily convey an attitude that college coaches will not find attractive. Discussing the financials with college coaches is appropriate, but only at the right time. You should always let the coach start the conversation regarding scholarships because the coach will eventually bring it up if you continue to communicate. This will also give you time to gather your thoughts about scholarships and prepare to respond to whatever the coach might throw at you. Timing and tone are key when discussing scholarship money with college soccer coaches.

"I'm a great fit for your program" [5.]

You may have cringed as you read this one but an optimistic player with a bit of confidence could easily make this mistake if they lack self-awareness. It's ultimately the coach's job to decide if you're a great fit for their program regardless of what you think. Let the way you play, the way you carry yourself, and your soccer brand communicate that you're a good fit for their program. This is much more attractive to college coaches.

Also, this statement can potentially indicate something wrong with a player's attitude. Players should realize that they won't be a good fit for every program and should be fine with that. Realize that you are ultimately only going to commit to one school. Today, high-profile American football players out high school send out a post on social media every time they get an offer. This builds up until they finally announce their commitment during a signing day event when everyone is watching. This is relevant because sometimes players just want offers for the sake of having the attention and affirmation. Club coaches and parents should encourage their players to be more mature than this and focus on the process rather than a glamorous end.

Bringing up past accomplishments very frequently

This one will annoy just about anyone other than your parents. Your discussions with college coaches are fundamentally prospective in nature. That being said, dwelling on the past already has you in the wrong frame of mind to effectively communicate your brand to college coaches. Possessing the right attitude toward the college soccer recruiting process is essential to set yourself up for success at the next level.

If a coach asks you about the level you've played at or your experience at a particular showcase then go ahead and speak honestly about it. What you shouldn't do is relate everything a coach says back to one of your past accomplishments.

In another more brutally honest sense, college coaches really don't care what you've accomplished in the past when you arrive on campus. You see this across all the highest levels of soccer. Anyone who has watched professional soccer for any length of time can name a handful of players who were on top of the world at one point and then completely fell from grace after a transfer to a new club. In short, don't make the mistake of dwelling in the past too long, as it will hinder your capacity to achieve your goals at the next level.

Should I pay someone to make my highlight tape?

The answer to this question really depends on what you can afford and how well you think you can use video editing software. If you have no idea how to begin using video editing software and think it will take you many hours that could be better spent doing school work, training, or working a part-time job then it might be better to get the film off one of your teammate's parents and pay someone else to make it for you. For those of you under a time crunch and want to get your video out quickly, paying someone might be a feasible option as well.

On the other hand, if you're already familiar with basic video editing then you might be better off doing it yourself. From Phase 3's discussion of highlight tapes, you know what should and should not be included in your highlight tape. With these two things you just need to put in the time to create it.

At the end of the day, it is better to have something rather than nothing for your highlight tape. Don't focus too much on making it perfect, who will make it, making it public vs. unlisted, etc. Rather, focus on what footage you do have and how you can maximize it to build your soccer brand.

Should a story of a bad college soccer experience deter me away from playing college soccer?

No. You absolutely should not let someone else's experience determine what you choose to do with your playing career. There are many parents and players that tell their poor experiences being part of a college soccer program. There may be several reasons for this. However, I find that one of the biggest is that players often have poor expectations for college soccer. For example, players expect school to easily take a backseat to athletics and that they will start every game and have a decent chance to move on to the professional ranks afterwards. Players often also expect that there will be less politics, less drama, and less poor refereeing in college soccer to name a few (none of these are true). Players with poor expectations and attitude will ultimately find themselves utterly disappointed with virtually any college soccer program.

Secondly, do not underestimate the ability for a player's lack of playing time to taint his experience in college soccer. Think about it. Most players go from being the star of their club team to working their tail off just to maybe be considered as a substitute. We see how professional players react in similar scenarios. Why would college soccer be any different? That being said, you should always consider the context in which someone tells his or her story.

Lastly, parents no longer have as much control when it comes to their kid and soccer. This is difficult for some parents who are too involved at the youth level and their only coping mechanism is to talk bad about the program and coach. While the coaching might actually be bad, it still does not negate the fact that such parents don't want to let go of the control or perception thereof they once had.

91

Notes

1. Steven Covey, *The 7 Habits of Highly Effective People* (New York: Simon and Schuster, 1989).

2. Michael Hyatt, Your Best Year Ever: A 5-Step Plan for Achieving Your Most Important Goals (Grand Rapids: Baker, 2018).

3. Matt Velazquez, "Wondolowski found the right fit at Cal State Chico," NCAA, June 18, 2013, http://www.ncaa.org/about/resources/media-center/news/wondolowski-found-right-fit-cal-state-chico

4. Dustin Hockensmith, "For Messiah College men's soccer program, the dynasty is in the details," Penn Live, December 23, 2013, https://www.pennlive.com/sports/2013/12/for_messiah_college_mens_socce.html

5. Christopher Roche, "The mistakes 90% of Athletes will make when talking with a College Coach," LinkedIn, June 4, 2018, https://www.linkedin.com/pulse/mistakes-90-athletes-make-when-talking-college-coach-roche/

More from the Author

For more content from Dennis about the recruiting process and other topics go to:

https://www.facebook.com/Soccercational/

Connect with him on social media:

Instagram: @denniswoodrowsparks

LinkedIn: https://www.linkedin.com/in/denniswoodrowsparks/

Made in the USA
Columbia, SC
10 August 2019